Dealing With Conflict & Anger

Edited by National Press Publications

NATIONAL PRESS PUBLICATIONS

A Division of Rockhurst University Continuing Education Center, Inc.

6901 West 63rd Street • P.O. Box 2949 • Shawnee Mission, Kansas 66201-1349

1-800-258-7248 • 1-913-432-7757

National Seminars endorses nonsexist language. In an effort to make this Business User's Manual clear, consistent and easy to read, we've used "he" throughout the odd-numbered chapters and "she" throughout the even-numbered chapters. The copy is not intended to be sexist.

Dealing With Conflict & Anger

Published by National Press Publications, Inc.
A Division of Rockhurst University Continuing Education Center, Inc.

Copyright 1996, National Press Publications

Printed in the United States of America

10

ISBN 1-55852-173-9

About Rockhurst University Continuing Education Center, Inc.

Rockhurst University Continuing Education Center, Inc., is committed to providing lifelong learning opportunities through the integration of innovative education and training.

National Seminars Group, a division of Rockhurst University Continuing Education Center, Inc., has its finger on the pulse of America's business community. We've trained more than 2 million people in every imaginable occupation to be more productive and advance their careers. Along the way, we've learned a few things. What it takes to be successful … how to build the skills to make it happen … and how to translate learning into results. Millions of people from thousands of companies around the world turn to National Seminars for training solutions.

National Press Publications is our product and publishing division. We offer a complete line of the finest self-study and continuous-learning resources available anywhere. These products present our industry-acclaimed curriculum and training expertise in a concise, action-oriented format you can put to work right away. Packed with real-world strategies and hands-on techniques, these resources are guaranteed to help you meet the career and personal challenges you face every day.

Legend Symbol Guide

 Exercises that reinforce your learning experience

 Questions that will help you apply the critical points to your situation

 Checklist that will help you identify important issues for future application

 Key issues to learn and understand for future application

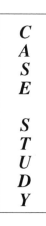 Real-world case studies that will help you apply the information you've learned

Contents

Introduction

You might think it's possible to get through your day without being faced with conflict, but think again! On any given day, your radio alarm wakes you to stories of a new war or relives overnight conflicts in your city that have left some citizens harmed. You hear your children arguing downstairs over the cereal or the TV channel. Driving to work, a motorist cuts you off, shouting and shaking his fist ... and you're not even at the office yet!

When you get there, it's likely there will be the usual disagreements. Some staff members just seem to dislike each other and clash regularly. Perhaps it's the interdepartmental disagreement left unresolved yesterday between the production and marketing departments ... or that "team" that seems to be at odds with itself again. Conflict seems to be as much a part of your life as the air you breathe.

It's easy to assume that conflict is bad, perhaps even evil. As a manager and as a human being, however, it's helpful to take a more balanced view of what conflict is in order to learn how to deal with it effectively.

Understanding conflict can help you:

1. Defuse your fear and reduce the sense of anxiety.

2. See clearly what it is and is not.

3. Manage negative events with confidence and skill.

4. Develop positive outcomes when conflict occurs, both in the workplace and in your relationships.

5. Create a cooperative atmosphere of team effort at the workplace.

> *Conflict seems to be as much a part of your life as the air you breathe.*

CHAPTER 1

Understanding Conflict and Anger

Conflict and Anger Are Part of Life

Conflict is neither good nor bad. Well-managed conflict can help your organization be creative and productive. Conflict offers the opportunity to learn. As Kenneth Kaye says, "If necessity is the mother of invention, conflict is its father." Conflict can provide an opportunity for personal growth and for greater effectiveness for a company.

Conflict Is Caused by Change

One of the few things you can count on in modern life is that things will change. This constant is one of the causes of conflict. It's easy to see why when you understand how every change sets off a series of predictable events. First, there is the change itself. (You move to another city.) Second, there is the resonance or echo each change event brings. (It reminded you of having to move when you were a teen and how you couldn't find new friends.) Third, there is the process you have to go through to adapt to the new change. This transition can take a long time if the change is significant — regardless of whether the change is something you want or not.

> *"If necessity is the mother of invention, conflict is its father."*
> Kenneth Kaye

This process of adjusting requires that you go through three steps. You must:

1. Let go of something familiar. This step is filled with fear, reluctance and resistance.

2. Go through a transition time: The old isn't workable any more and the new isn't yet comfortable. Anxiety is usually quite high during this step. Many people will lash out in anger during this period of discomfort.

3. Adjust to a new way of doing things. As individuals adjust to change, a time of awkward attempts and tentative steps can be expected. Those with a healthy self-esteem generally tolerate their own mistakes and forge ahead to new comfort zones.

Because change is occurring in many parts of your life, you rarely have time to adjust and completely settle down between changes. At any point in time you are juggling more than one stage in the change process.

What does this have to do with conflict?

Dealing with many changes and with continual change creates stress, tension and anxiety. Multiply that times the number of people in your workplace and tension develops, patience runs short and people lose sight of the bigger picture and become self-focused. All of this causes — you guessed it — conflict!

The Chinese symbol for conflict is a combination of two Chinese words: danger and opportunity. Conflict doesn't necessarily mean there's an impending disaster but includes a possible positive opportunity.

The Chinese symbol for conflict is a combination of two Chinese words: danger and opportunity. You may find it helpful to think of conflict as neither positive nor negative. This symbol provides a new, neutral label for conflict. Conflict doesn't necessarily mean there's an impending disaster but includes a possible positive opportunity.

In this book you will learn to understand conflict and anger, acquire specific skills to deal with anger in yourself as a person and as a manager and learn skills to deal with the conflict and anger of others.

Exercise

Describe in each area of your life changes that are occurring and which of the three steps you are on.

Work relationships _____
_____
_____

Parents _____
_____
_____

Children _____
_____
_____

Volunteer activities _____
_____
_____

Projects you manage _____
_____
_____

Church _____
_____
_____

Other _____
_____
_____
_____
_____

How Conflict and Anger Work

What Conflict Is

Each of us is familiar with the experience of conflict and anger. But what are they? Conflict is defined in different ways: as a fight, a battle, a disagreement, a difference of opinion or ideas, a misunderstanding. How would you define it? In the workplace, conflict most often centers around a difference of opinion. These differences are not always negative, but it's the negative ones we tend to remember!

What Anger Is

Can you remember the last time you felt angry? Perhaps it was today at home or at work. Did you feel mildly angry? Did you feel intensely angry and lose your temper or feel like you wanted to strike out? Unlike conflict, anger is a *feeling*. It is a feeling of hurt or displeasure from injury, mistreatment, misunderstanding or opposition. At times anger leads to an uncontrolled outburst. Any time you express anger in a destructive way, you've lost control. What many people fail to realize is that while you may lose control, it is possible to learn to control your angry behavior and feelings.

In order to manage anger, you first need to learn how to control this emotion. In fact, control is the key. Understanding how your emotions and behaviors are connected is the first step in exercising control. The diagram below illustrates this relationship.

FEAR/ANGER

Reprinted with permission from "How to Handle Conflict and Manage Anger," page 1, copyright 1992, Rockhurst College Continuing Education Center, Inc., Overland Park, KS.

> *"A man is what he thinks about all day long."*
> Ralph Waldo Emerson

Three Emotional Dimensions of Conflict

Why You Get Angry

Beyond your primary needs of food, clothing and shelter, there are three other needs all of us share:

1. The need to be loved, valued and appreciated.
2. The need to be in control — of ourselves and our destinies.
3. The need for self-esteem.

1. *Every person wants to feel important and valued.* It is not only young children who have this need. Throughout our entire lives we have this need in varying degrees. None of us ever outgrows our basic human need for love.

   This basic need may emerge at work when we feel left out, e.g., being excluded from an important meeting, or when we believe we have something valuable to contribute and no one asks our opinion.

2. *We all want to have control of our lives,* but a good deal of your life is controlled by the clock, by another's expectations, by schedules and by plans made for us by a boss, spouse, parent, friend or even society. Whether you travel to work on the subway, the freeway or the plane, just getting there puts you in someone else's control. Yet we have a need to control some aspects of our lives. Always living under someone else's control is both debilitating and intolerable.

3. *Self-esteem is a basic ego need.* Feeling good about ourselves is an essential need we all share. Feeling a sense of self-worth is the foundation for self-confidence, and the greater your self-confidence, the greater your ability to control anger and conflict.

   Whenever you feel you're in danger of losing one of these needs or having them threatened, you may react emotionally with fear or anger.

> *"As long as you blame your anger on someone else ... you give up the chance to change how you respond."*
> Hendrie Weisinger

Fear, Anger or Self-Control

When emotion is directed inward — it is *fear*. When it's directed outward — it is *anger*.

Both of these emotions are what we call accountable emotions — they are reactions to people or situations that you choose. As surprising as that may seem to you, it works very simply:

Feelings arise from thoughts.
I create my own thoughts.
Therefore, I choose my feelings.

Others do not control your anger, you do. The good news is that just as you can choose to be angry, you can choose not to be angry. Understanding how this works will teach you how to take responsibility for your emotions and control them.

> *"If we manage conflict constructively, we harness its energy for creativity and development."*
> Kenneth Kaye

Here's an example that illustrates how our thoughts can not only control but actually change a negative emotion into a productive event. Several months ago a small commuter flight we were aboard encountered some pretty severe turbulence. One passenger pulled out her briefcase and began to work, seemingly oblivious to the bumps and bounces. Another passenger toward the front of the plane was "white-knuckling" the seat, shouting "Oh my God" with every bump.

Same plane, same turbulence, but very different outcomes!

How do you react when you feel afraid or when you feel angry? No doubt you respond in one of the following ways:

1. *Retaliation:* This is when you decide to get even, to "get back" at someone. Children do this by "telling," ostracizing, hitting, etc. How do people in your office retaliate?

2. *Domination:* This is when you react by yelling or screaming. Children do this by name-calling or shouting at each other. Some dominate through their job title, and others can dominate through their physical stature.

3. *Isolation:* This is when you withdraw, sulk or pout. In children we see: "I'm going to take my toys and go home." Do you know someone at work who uses this method?

4. *Coping:* This is when you collaborate or use your skills to manage the situation. When have you reacted to a conflict in this way ... working out the problem with yourself, with another person or persons?

All four of these reactions are options you can use, and each produces its own unique outcome. To effectively manage anger, you must first decide what outcome you want. Coping, of course is the preferable path and the one for which you'll develop skills as you go through this book.

Remember: You choose your reaction to any situation. Your reactions are not forced on you by circumstances over which you have no power.

Before you learn how to control your emotions during conflict, you can assess how you are likely to deal with anger in conflict by using the test on the next page.

Let's get a picture of how you might react in situations in which conflict and anger are likely to arise. Then, with that knowledge, you can begin to build skills and learn to control situations.

Read through the following 25 statements. After thinking about each situation, rate on a scale of 1 to 5 the level of volatility of your reaction, circling your response. On this scale, 1 indicates a relatively calm reaction and 5 indicates a major eruption. The more honest you can be with each situation, the more accurate will be the results. Get in touch with your normal, natural responses.

> *"A pot with the lid on comes to a boil faster — and boils over."*
> Kenneth Kaye

Volatility Assessment

1. As you're leaving for an appointment, you spill coffee on your clothing.   1 2 3 4 5

2. A car pulls out in front of you, causing you to slam on your brakes, and the other driver gestures at you as if you'd done something wrong.   1 2 3 4 5

3. You miss a deadline at work because information to be supplied by someone else arrives late.   1 2 3 4 5

4. A waiter gets your order wrong, and you're served a meal you don't want.   1 2 3 4 5

5. Friends arrive unexpectedly, assuming you're ready to entertain them.   1 2 3 4 5

6. You must wait an extremely long time at a medical or dental office.   1 2 3 4 5

7. You drop a gallon of milk, spilling it all over the floor.   1 2 3 4 5

8. You're driving behind a car going 10 miles an hour under the legal speed limit, and there is no way you can pass.   1 2 3 4 5

9. You get a ticket for parking illegally.   1 2 3 4 5

10. Someone makes fun of your new haircut.   1 2 3 4 5

11. At work, you're criticized by your boss in front of several colleagues.   1 2 3 4 5

12. At the last minute, a friend cancels out of plans you'd made for the evening.   1 2 3 4 5

13. Someone takes credit for work you did.   1 2 3 4 5

14. You discover that someone is spreading gossip about you.   1 2 3 4 5

15. Someone you're speaking to doesn't even pretend to be listening to you.   1 2 3 4 5

16. A friend borrows something of yours — car, book, clothing, etc. — and returns it damaged, though he or she makes no mention of its condition.   1 2 3 4 5

17. Your judgment or intelligence is called into question.   1 2 3 4 5

18. A pen breaks in the pocket of your favorite suit.   1 2 3 4 5

19. An expensive item of clothing returns from the cleaners with a large stain.   1 2 3 4 5

20. Someone at work goes through your desk drawers without your permission.   1 2 3 4 5

21. At the very last minute, you are asked to make a presentation at work on a subject with which you are unfamiliar.   1 2 3 4 5

22. Your spouse or partner makes a major purchase without consulting you.   1 2 3 4 5

23. Friends bring their toddler to your home and sit silently as the child wreaks havoc on your belongings.   1 2 3 4 5

24. Despite your certainty, you are unable to convince your bank that they have made an error adversely affecting your balance.   1 2 3 4 5

25. A friend tells someone personal information you shared in confidence.   1 2 3 4 5

After answering all the questions, add the numbers you have circled. Place your total score in the blank below.

Total Score: _____

Scoring:

If your total score is:

25 - 50: While there is probably always room for improvement, you remain admirably calm in the face of potentially vexing situations. You have learned that there are other options besides anger as a reaction to change and sudden or unpleasant developments. The rest of this book will help you refine your already praiseworthy ability to remain cool and in control.

51-100: If you scored in this range, join the club. This is where the majority of people taking this self-assessment find themselves before making use of the coping strategies in this book. Your ability to contain conflict and anger at a generally manageable and non-destructive level still needs work. You opt for anger more than you should.

101-125: You are literally in the process of killing yourself. Your volcanic reactions to life's difficult situations harm your body and health. It is probable that, in the past, you have jeopardized friendships and working relationships — if not lost them altogether. It is vital that you pay attention to the lessons in the chapters ahead.

Myths About Conflict

There are certain myths about conflict that can cloud our judgment and cause us to act ineffectively. Let's look at some of these myths or false assumptions. Once you understand them you will be much more skillful in dealing with conflict and anger when they occur. When you lack understanding about something, it has power over you. The opposite is also true: greater knowledge and understanding give us power. Let's give you some power right now by exploring these myths!

Five Myths That Prevent Positive Conflict Management

1. Conflict is a product of poor management.
2. Conflict is a sign of low concern for the organization.
3. Anger is negative and destructive.
4. Conflict, if left alone, will take care of itself.
5. Conflict must be resolved immediately.

Myth #1: Conflict is a product of poor management

Do you question your management skills or the skill of others because staff members are experiencing conflict? Maybe if you were a better manager, there wouldn't be so much conflict among your employees. This myth feeds on low self-esteem and insecurity, and pulls a manager into a cycle of fear and worry. The fact is, conflict happens. As an effective manager you can anticipate conflict when possible, deal with conflict when it does arise and enjoy its absence on those rare occasions when things are running smoothly.

One quality that made the great horseman Willie Shoemaker an extraordinary jockey was his excellent control. The horse, often unaware of his presence, never felt his hand on the rein unless it was needed. As a good manager you have to strive for a "soft set of hands" like Willie Shoemaker during conflict.

Tension will naturally arise as your business relationships are stretched to their limit. Your effectiveness as a manager improves when you respond with the "soft hands" of conflict management, neither judging nor being judged by the presence of conflict.

In some cases a workplace may *appear* to lack conflict. That means either:

A. Conflict is being managed and is not apparent to outsiders.

B. Conflict is hidden and will eventually surface at a more serious level.

As a manager or supervisor you are not to be blamed for the presence of conflict. Conflict exists wherever people interact. In fact, people who are dedicated and committed to reaching their goals will often collide with one another, not because they are poorly managed but because they are so well focused they want to hit their targets.

Remember: You will be judged by how you manage the conflict, not by the *presence* of it!

> *"Arguing is a game that two can play at. But it is a strange game in that neither opponent ever wins."*
> Benjamin Franklin

Myth #2: Conflict is a sign of low concern for the organization

Actually, the opposite is often true. People indicate what is important to them by what they are willing to fight for. The extent to which you are willing to fight for something reflects how strongly you feel about it. A line worker who becomes angry at shoddy work can be reacting out of concern for a quality product.

Remember: Conflict can help clarify emotions and identify underlying values. Sometimes it is only when you are challenged by a situation that you discover how important it really is to you.

Have you ever been surprised that you had such a strong reaction to something? That could be your inner self revealing that this is something you care about more than you realized.

Myth #3: Anger is negative and destructive

This myth ignores anger as an emotion which, like others, is neither positive nor negative. Anger can be negative and destructive, of course, but it doesn't have to be. Its impact is determined by what you do with it. Like conflict, anger can also be a sign of caring.

Remember: Anger can lead to satisfaction and can improve a situation if you deal with it appropriately.

Myth #4: Conflict, if left alone, will take care of itself

This is a half-truth. You can avoid conflict — and sometimes that is a valid strategy — but avoidance is not the only strategy and is not always a good strategy to use. Conflict can escalate as easily as it can dissipate, but when it is not acknowledged, it may take on a life of its own. Ignoring conflict allows it to grow out of proportion through gossip, innuendo and inaction.

Remember: Left unchecked, conflict can escalate as easily and quickly as it can dissipate. Maybe quicker!

> *"Problems are messages."*
> Shakti Gawain

Myth #5: Conflict must be resolved immediately

This is the counterpart to Myth #4. On the one hand, certain types of conflict will grow if left alone; however, solving other types of conflict too quickly can mean you don't get the best solution. In this case, the underlying need is not problem-solving but the desire to eliminate the unpleasant environment of the conflict as quickly as possible and restore at least the appearance of peace. If you slow down and take the time to define the conflict accurately and examine a variety of options, you'll increase your chances of finding the best solution. A conflict well defined is a conflict half solved.

Remember: It's OK to slow down when you're evaluating a conflict. Premature resolution can limit your options.

Recognizing and naming these five myths weakens their control over you and gives you more confidence and power. When you are held captive by their power, you are not free to be an effective conflict manager. Understanding is the first step in gaining the power to cope with the ever-present conflict we face.

Exercise

Identify the two myths you find most likely to creep into your conflicts.

1. _____

_____

2. _____

_____

What is one way you can use the information about myths in your own work situation? _____

_____

_____

Maintaining Self-Control

You have learned that anger and fear are emotional reactions you can choose in a conflict situation or when your basic needs are threatened. Also understand that neither anger nor fear is very productive in getting those needs met.

You can more successfully handle any conflict you face when you:

- Control your emotions.
- Control the facts.

Are these two techniques easy? Not always. But here is a four-step system, each step represented by a question, that will help you stay cool, calm and in control, at least most of the time.

The first step in controlling your emotions is to ask yourself the following four questions:

1. What past experiences were similar to this situation, and what did I learn from them? *(Projection)*
2. What is my level of commitment to this person/situation? *(Relationship)*
3. What other factors are influencing my thinking/this situation? *(Present event)*
4. What do I stand to lose? *(Risk)*

Now let's look at the issues each question raises:

1. **Projection:** What past experiences were like this, and what did I learn from them?

   Sometimes your reaction to an event triggers a stronger emotion than it should. This happens when it is echoing or reminding you of a situation you've experienced in the past. Facing this head-on will enable you to keep your emotions in perspective and help you understand what's really going on and how to maintain your self-control. Ask yourself: Why am I really this upset? Is it because of what's happening now, or am I projecting from another experience?

> *"You become a worrier by practicing worry. You become free of worry by practicing the opposite."*
> Norman Vincent Peale

13

It is rare that you have an experience totally different from or unrelated to previous life experiences. In fact, you may be experiencing essentially the same conflict you've been through before. One thing is generally true — unresolved conflict emerges again! It may be with a different person or in a different situation, but it's the same conflict.

Drawing on your past experiences can put you a step ahead in the coping process. Use the wisdom of these past experiences and the knowledge you gained, first to control your emotions and secondly to view your current problem more objectively.

Scenario: You are stuck in traffic on the way to meet with an important client. You become angry and upset. Are you projecting past experiences? Where did the anger spring from? What have you learned from your past experience? You've been late before and the client got upset and uncooperative. You felt uncomfortable and you don't want to feel that uncomfortable again.

2. **Relationship:** What is my level of commitment to this person/ situation?

Your reaction to conflict will depend on the relationship you have with the person or situation (a job, for instance). If the relationship is not important or is relatively unimportant, your level of commitment and concern will usually be lower. We tend to discount, and even ignore, opinions and ideas of those we do not respect.

In the scenario above, your relationship is with an important client. You have a professional commitment. If you were stuck in traffic on the way to the doctor for a routine checkup and were happy to be out on the road on a beautiful afternoon, the same traffic jam would not as likely trigger your anger. You'd know that it was not critical to be there on time and that you could reschedule if necessary.

> *"You can observe a lot by watching."*
> Yogi Berra

3. **Present Event:** What other factors are influencing my thinking/ this situation?

   This is the most important step to consider because every event is part of the larger picture of what is going on in your life. Each of us lives in a kind of bubble in which all the things happening in our lives rub together and impact each other. One annoyance contributes to your reaction to the next thing. Getting a raise makes the next problem your supervisor brings you seem manageable. Staying up all night with a sick child sets you up to overreact to problems at work. Life is an enormous jigsaw puzzle.

Each of us lives in a kind of bubble in which all the things happening in our lives rub together and impact each other.

4. **Risk:** What do I stand to lose?

   This is the question that helps you put today's conflict in perspective. Another way of asking this question is to say, "Is this worth getting upset about? What does it matter in the big picture of my life? How important is it in the long run?"

Analyzing a situation using these four questions helps you understand your emotional reactions and get them under control. In the process, it provides you with useful knowledge about:

1. What have I learned in the past that is helpful here?
2. Is this worth being upset about?
3. Is this really what's upsetting me, or am I upset about other things and blowing it out of proportion?
4. How important is this in the big picture?

Life is an enormous jigsaw puzzle.

Current Conflict in Your Life

Think about a current conflict and fill in the following lines, using the four questions from the previous page. Briefly define the conflict in the space provided, and then analyze it using the four questions.

1. Projection: What past experiences were like this situation, and what did I learn from them?

   Experience: _____

   _____

   _____

   _____

2. Relationship: What is my level of commitment to this person/situation?

   _____

   _____

   _____

3. Present Event: What other factors are influencing my thinking/this situation?

   _____

   _____

   _____

4. Risk: What do I stand to lose?

   _____

   _____

   _____

When you automatically stop and ask these four questions about a conflict, you will find that the emotions of conflict in your life can be controlled. This kind of self-talk is worth the practice!

Anger Management: Who Owns the Problem?

Another important step in dealing with conflict and anger effectively is to identify who really owns the problem. Sometimes, in the midst of anger, the issue of ownership is confused, and the angry party ends up having more than his share of the problem because he becomes the problem.

The following is a model for placing ownership of the problem where it belongs:

I have a problem **1**	We have a problem **2**
3 They have a problem	**4** There is no problem

> *Sometimes, in the midst of anger, the issue of ownership is confused, and the angry party ends up having more than his share of the problem because he becomes the problem.*

In the *first quadrant,* the problem is important only to you. You alone are responsible for finding a solution, and the matter really doesn't affect anyone else. The work is getting done and life is going on. Recognize and accept it when the problem is yours — then dig in and fix it!

Your best strategy is to isolate the issues and do your best to separate emotion from facts. If you own the problem, don't look for someone to rescue you or share the burden. If you find yourself in this quadrant, become tactical and strategic — move forward toward a solution that satisfies you. After all, it's your problem.

In the *second quadrant*, the problem extends beyond yourself. Here, we have a problem. This is a different situation from the first. Results are not being produced and we need to define the problem, address it and negotiate a solution together. The burden for a solution is shared.

When "we" share a problem, the burden shifts toward mutually satisfactory resolution. The best course of action when "we" own the problem is to seek mutual benefit areas. It's usually unproductive to focus on the points of disagreement; instead look for points of commonality. Mutually beneficial aspects of the disagreement can always be identified if you let go of the debatable issues for a while. Research indicates that in most conflict, you can find 85 percent agreement.

In the ***third quadrant***, the problem belongs to someone else. As a manager or supervisor you may often find your employees trying to move the problem from themselves to you. This is sometimes called "upward delegation" or "putting the monkey on your back." Has anyone ever done this to you? One of the first things managers need to learn is how to teach employees to accept responsibility for their problems. It is safer for them to have you solve their problem than to risk solving it themselves. However, if you solve it, they will make you responsible for all their problems. Soon you'll spend your time doing their work and not yours. In addition, when they fail, you'll be blamed.

As an effective supervisor, you show leadership by consistently empowering your staff to take responsibility. When someone brings you a problem, ask, "What do you think? What solutions have you come up with?" rather than providing solutions for them. Then allow your employees to fail without retaliation so they may learn and grow. Help them by listening, asking questions, encouraging and praising. Remember, taking on their problems is not helping them. It is keeping them dependent.

In the ***fourth quadrant***, there is no problem. Many times, big conflicts aren't the result of a specific problem at all. People may have gotten upset based on their own perception or misperception of reality. Part of a supervisor's role is to help workers see things from a broader point of view so conflicts over imaginary problems don't occur.

During conflict, it is often a bad strategy to openly share one's feelings, but when there is no problem … share your feelings! Talk openly and honestly about what's on your mind, and since there is *no* problem — keep anger in check.

> *"The passion for setting people right is in itself an afflictive disease."*
> Marianne Moore

A Reality Check

There are three possible ways to perceive reality:

1. ***How you see things.*** Based on your past experiences and conditioning, everything that has happened to you in your entire life has led you to believe that this is the way the world works.

2. ***How others see things.*** Based on their past experience and conditioning, which are usually different from yours, everything that has ever happened to them has led them to believe that this is the way the world should work.

3. ***How things really are.*** If you try to achieve this perspective whenever possible, you'll have the best chance of success in problem-solving.

As a manager you adopt the third perspective when you're dealing with problems between and among staff members. Your job at that point is akin to a traffic officer who has come upon an accident and is writing a report. You need to get around the emotions in order to discover what really happened. What are the facts? What happened? Who is involved? To whom does the problem belong?

EXERCISE

In the space provided below, identify a recent or ongoing conflict or an anger-producing situation. Explore the question of ownership. Figure out to whom the problem belongs and determine your best course of action. Did you see it that way at the time?

Problem/Situation _____

_____

Who owns the problem? _____

Why do you say that? _____

_____

How does assigning ownership to this (these) person(s) change the way you view the problem or situation? _____

_____

Knowing the problem's ownership, how much of an emotional investment do you have in the situation? _____

_____

Emotional Aspects of Conflict

You come to work in the morning happy as a clam and the phone rings before you're settled at your desk. The call is from an important customer who begins screaming at you about how incompetent you are. How do you feel inside?

One of your peers comes to talk with you about his proposal that you've just read. You have some problems with the way it will affect your department. Inviting you to lunch, he suggests it might be a good time to see how you can work out your differences. How do you feel inside?

Two of your supervisers have been involved in a simmering disagreement for some weeks, and you've been hoping they would work it out. You see them glaring at each other in the coffee room as you walk in. What do you feel at that moment?

Inside and Outside

When you feel angry on the inside, you react in some way on the outside. In fact, what happens inside you when you feel angry has a big impact on what happens outside. When someone says something hurtful or challenging to you, your emotions can cause you to react in a number of ways. Understanding what's going on with your emotions when you're in conflict will help you maintain control and take care of the problem in a healthy and helpful manner. Let's look at the three emotional dynamics in any conflict:

1. The Rejection Response
2. The Interpersonal Gap
3. Emotional Rebounding

> *"When organizational norms discourage the expression of 'weakness' such as hurt, fear, sadness or shame, people are more likely to substitute aggressive feelings (jealousy, anger, desire for revenge) and to escalate disputes."*
> Kenneth Kaye

The Rejection Response

People follow a predictable sequence as they try to deal with the emotional aspects of conflict.

Step 1. Anxiety
Step 2. Acceptance
Step 3. A Journey Inward
  • Flight
  • Fight
Step 4. A Balanced Reflection

Step 1: Anxiety.   Our first reaction to sudden change or challenge is anxiety. For some people it's a feeling in the pit of their stomachs; for others it's a fast heartbeat or sweaty palms. Anxiety is a natural response during conflict. Some people hide their response; others become transparent.

Our anxiety is often driven by fear. The fear response, as old as humanity, can certainly move you to act! When your employees are displaying anxiety, your emotional radar tells you things are at the first step in a conflict.

Step 2: Acceptance. Between anxiety and acceptance there is a chasm. Many conflicts never make it across this chasm. One option in a conflict is to walk away (or run away), to reject the other party. Did you ever have a friendship tested by a conflict and decide to just stop being friends?   Watching children dealing with disagreements, you hear them say, "Well, all right, I'm not going to be your friend anymore!" And they pick up their toys and go home. Of course, with children, they are often back together again the next day.

Volunteer organizations tend to lose people at this step. It's easier to volunteer someplace else than to deal with the conflict or the change people face. The relationship is not strong enough, not worth the effort to work through the conflict. A more desirable conclusion in any organization is an acceptance that things can be worked out, that our conflicts can be dealt with and that the people and the end product are worth the struggle.

When you get people to move away from blame, you can move them toward acceptance. Sometimes this happens very slowly with employees, but once a level of acceptance is reached, the next step follows quite naturally. It is helpful to work on building relationships and to keep focusing on the problem rather than on the person.

Step 3: A Journey Inward. Taking a journey inward involves getting in touch with what is going on inside yourself, taking a personal inventory. You decide which is better: fight or flight. Is this the time to stand up for your values and concerns or to retreat and wait for a better time? Conflict presents these two possibilities at this phase.

> *"Three of the key elements in the art of working together are how to deal with change, how to deal with conflict and how to reach our potential."*
> Max DuPree

At this point it is important to listen ... listen to your instincts and pay attention to the intensity of your feelings. As you learn to manage inner emotions, you will grow as a person and as a manager.

How can you use this inner journey to help turn your negative emotions into positive affirmations? Here are four ways:

1. **Cherish the freedom to be you.** Affirm that you are worthwhile whether you are raging or calm.
2. **Identify negative feelings before they are expressed.** Body language is an excellent signal. Listen carefully, discern wisely and focus consciously. Be aware of your anger.
3. **Trust yourself.** Feel, speak and act spontaneously. Go with the flow until you find it ineffective or unsatisfying. Trust your instincts.
4. **Own your thoughts, feelings, words and actions.** Others don't make you angry. You choose to be angry. Own your anger.

Step 4: Balanced Reflection. With a balanced perspective you understand that running from the issues means continually running; the fighting never stops. A conflict can only be resolved by acknowledging and analyzing it. This type of balanced reflection is a reminder that if conflicts simmer unattended, they are likely to escalate. Balanced reflection allows you to lower the level of intensity, and doing so makes it easier to address the conflict and manage whatever the problem is.

23

The Rejection Response is a quick look at the emotional aspects of conflict. While the business manager is not a psychologist, understanding these emotional dynamics gives you a means of understanding what is happening inside everyone involved. As a manager, one of your most important roles is to provide perspective. Learning to "read" the emotional climate of a conflict allows you to do that.

The Interpersonal Gap: Communication

The second emotional factor, communication, is typically a major problem during conflict. Many issues could be resolved if communication was improved. From an emotional perspective, the loss of communication compounds problems as the parties in conflict begin to project what they "believe" are the other side's motivations. This gap between the intended message and internally received messages contributes to communication problems during conflict.

The Interpersonal Gap

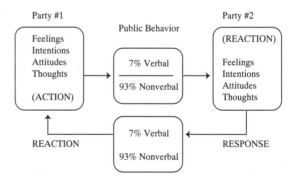

Reprinted with permission from *How to Manage Conflict* by Dr. William Hendricks, copyright 1991, National Press Publications, Overland Park, KS.

> *"In fluid and turbulent times, it is better to think in terms of coping with conflicts than resolving them."*
> Roger Fisher

As the chart above shows, only 7 percent of communication is verbal. The rest is nonverbal, including facial expressions, body language and the tone of voice a person uses. A communication gap arises during conflict as parties struggle to match others' words and actions. Keep in mind the following points as you assess a conflict.

1. Words improperly used or vain attempts to spare another's feelings fall into this interpersonal gap. When an emotion does not match the explanation, the possibility for conflict and misunderstanding increases greatly.

2. There is a relationship between input and feedback. If you send positive messages, you'll get positive feedback. If you send negative messages, you'll get negative feedback. (When your bank teller has just waited on an extremely rude and argumentative customer, you know you may get the brunt of his frustration if you're next in line. However, if you take a minute to empathize with him and compliment him on his patience, the chances are high that he will treat you courteously.)

3. When you, as a manager, help your employees communicate clearly and calmly, you have given them a vital tool to use in avoiding and dealing with conflicts.

Here are five tips to build communication during conflict:

Tip #1: Ask clarifying questions before you formulate a response. It's hard to disengage a wrong assumption once it's spoken. For example: "Bill, that sounds interesting; let me clarify what I heard before I respond, OK?"

> *When your bank teller has just waited on an extremely rude, argumentative customer, you know you may get the brunt of his frustration if you're next in line.*

Tip #2: Isolate the positive points before you disagree. Find the points of mutual benefit by listening for things you like or agree with. Example: "I really like what you said about. ... Can we explore that further?"

Tip #3: Remove the bite before you bark. Negative attitudes and criticism create emotional and personal threats when they are spoken with anger or emotion. Develop the habit of talking about your feelings and your concerns before you attack what "they" said or did. Example: "I'm really frustrated right now and unsure of where to begin. Can we step back one step and discuss how we got to this place before we argue about a solution?"

Tip #4: Remember, understanding someone's position does not mean you agree. Saying something like "I really want to understand your ideas. Can you elaborate?" opens up the information channel. You'll have plenty of time to disagree later if you need to.

Tip #5: Don't die on every hill. It's good business to lose once in a while, or you'll simply be cut out of the communication loop. If you always win, soon other people will play elsewhere.

A more useful question than "Who is right?" is: "How can we move forward?"

Emotional Rebounding

When conflict escalates away from cooperation, emotional rebounding or turning backward occurs. Let's look at what this means for you. Emotional rebounding has three elements:

1. Blaming
2. Secrecy
3. Repressed feelings and anger

1. ***Blaming.*** When blaming occurs, the focus is not on finding a solution to the problem, because employees are bogged down in finger pointing or defending themselves. Blaming also involves personal attacks, which compound the original problem and make it harder to work together for a solution. Do you hear: "It's her fault; she should have ..." "Our department didn't do it." "You should/shouldn't have ..." In each of these examples, the problem is not being addressed. Rather, people are placing blame through personal attacks. This keeps everyone from solving the problem and builds anger and resentment.

2. ***Secrecy.*** Secrecy is another element of emotional rebounding. When secrecy comes into play, facts go underground, and at a time they are most needed. Secrecy is characterized by an inability to remain neutral. People become very protective of their information and their loyalties. Secrecy heightens any conflict and quickly plunges people into "camps."

As a manager you may be able to identify with this point. People are quick to blame but slow to "rat" on a fellow employee. Rumors run rampant, but facts go into hiding and stifle the resolution efforts. Secrecy keeps problems from being solved, and it becomes a powerful distraction.

3. *Repressed Feelings and Anger.* Feelings are repressed when those involved believe that feelings are bad and emotions should be held back. When anger is vented during lower-level conflicts, catharsis happens. The conflict is out and over with, and you know how people feel. The feelings also make it easy to identify issues and values involved. But as conflict escalates, venting feelings is more dangerous. When anger is expressed during more serious stages of conflict, it has the opposite effect!

Emotional rebounding causes us to use our emotions in exactly the wrong way. Because we try to get along at low stages of conflict, we bury our emotions. When conflict rises, we lose it! You can learn to change this habit and, as a manager, give "permission" to your people to express anger before a conflict has escalated. (Note: Personal attacks should never be condoned. Instead, people may express their anger over issues, situations or specific behaviors.)

When anger does surface at the higher stages of conflict, one excellent management technique is to say, "It is clear that everyone is angry, but it will help us little to escalate our emotions. I recognize your anger and will seriously consider your concerns. There is no longer a need to vent those emotions in this setting."

> *"Understanding how others view a problem gives us strength. It enhances our ability to influence them."*
> Roger Fisher

Emotional Issues Checklist

Directions: On the line below, think of a recent conflict and describe it briefly. Then read each statement below, rating yourself on the continuum.

1 = I neglected to do this   5 = I did extremely well

Creating a Safe Environment/Situation

1. I shared hope and optimism.   1   2   3   4   5

2. I communicated that this problem is
    manageable.   1   2   3   4   5

3. I made it clear that no one needs to be
    hurt.   1   2   3   4   5

4. I communicated a concern for everyone's
    success.   1   2   3   4   5

5. I established equality: 1   2   3   4   5
    • Put-downs/personal attacks were not
      allowed
    • No reprimands were given for
      expressing honest opinions
    • All feelings were acceptable

6. I communicated that all involved will
    survive.   1   2   3   4   5

Meeting the Needs of Others
1. I communicated, "I care about you."   1   2   3   4   5

2. I communicated, "I care about our
    relationship."   1   2   3   4   5

3. I communicated, "I care about this
    company."   1   2   3   4   5

4. I communicated, "I want you to have
    some input in how this will be resolved." 1   2   3   4   5

Joining the Issue ... Inviting ... Confronting

1. I used statements such as: 1 2 3 4 5
   "We (not you) have a problem."
   "Let's get started together."

2. I listened to the facts.   1 2 3 4 5

3. I listened to the feelings.   1 2 3 4 5

4. I separated fact from opinion.   1 2 3 4 5

5. I looked for multiple solutions.   1 2 3 4 5

> *Give "permission" to your people to express anger before a conflict has escalated.*

Scoring: As a manager, you must teach people the skills of conflict management. Start by allowing conflict to surface in a safe and productive manner. A score below 40 indicates that you probably are not helping yourself or others move toward resolution.

Questions for Personal Development

1. What is the major emphasis of this chapter?

_____

_____

_____

_____

2. What are the most important things you learned from this chapter?

_____

_____

_____

_____

3. How can you apply what you learned to your current job?

_____

_____

_____

_____

4. How will you go about making these improvements?

_____

_____

_____

_____

5. How can you monitor improvement?

_____

_____

_____

_____

6. Summarize the changes you expect to see in yourself one year from now.

_____

_____

_____

_____

CHAPTER 2

Conflict: Danger or Opportunity?

Your Conflict Management Style

Did you ever wonder why some people act one way and you act completely differently in the same situation? Do you know someone who just naturally seems at ease handling conflict and wonder why you aren't more like that? Who you are today is an accumulation of your past life experiences combined with your conscious decisions. You hardly ever act without being influenced by your background, your experience and your personal history with conflict. These things all affect how you approach other people when you meet them for the first time, how you organize your social life, how you interact with others at work and, of course, how you deal with conflict. Understanding how you tend to deal with conflict is a self-revelation that is very empowering.

Knowing yourself is the first major step in gaining personal control in conflict situations.

So, how do you act when you find yourself embroiled in a conflict? Completing the exercise on the next page will help you clarify your behavior. This information will also be useful in learning how to flex your style and use different styles to handle different types of conflict. As you do this exercise, remember that the more honestly your answers represent how you really handle

> *"The times in my life when I feel the worst are those times when I've not been true to myself."*
> Abraham Lincoln

31

conflict, the more helpful this exercise will be to you. To accomplish this, imagine your work situation and the people you typically deal with when you choose each answer.

Here are 10 conflict situations, each with five resolution alternatives. Rank your answers in the order of how well they describe you.

Place a 5 next to your first choice, a 4 next to your second choice and a 3 next to your third choice. Don't rank anything with a 2 or a 1. You'll have two unused completions for each statement. Remember: you'll write a 5, a 4 and a 3 next to your first, second and third choices, respectively.

EXERCISE

1. When you have strong feelings in a conflict situation, you:
   _____ A. Enjoy the emotional release and sense of exhilaration and accomplishment.
   _____ B. Enjoy the challenge of the conflict.
   _____ C. Find it frightening because someone will get hurt.
   _____ D. Become convinced there is nothing you can do to resolve the issue.
   _____ E. Become serious and concerned about how others are feeling and thinking.

2. The best result you can expect from a conflict is:
   _____ A. To help people face facts.
   _____ B. To cancel out extremes in thinking so a strong middle ground can be reached.
   _____ C. To demonstrate the absurdity of self-centeredness and draw people closer together.
   _____ D. To lessen complacency and assign blame where it belongs.
   _____ E. To clear the air and enhance commitment and results.

3. When you have authority in a conflict situation, you:
   _____ A. Put it straight and let others know your view.
   _____ B. Try to negotiate the best settlement.
   _____ C. Go along with the others, providing support where you can.
   _____ D. Keep the encounter impersonal, citing rules if they apply.
   _____ E. Ask for other viewpoints and suggest that a position be found that both sides might try.

2

4. When someone takes an unreasonable position, you:
___ A. Lay it on the line and say that you don't like it.
___ B. Let her know in casual, subtle ways that you're not pleased, possibly distract with humor and avoid direct confrontation.
___ C. Keep your misgivings to yourself.
___ D. Let your actions speak for you, possibly using depression or lack of interest.
___ E. Call attention to the conflict and explore mutually acceptable solutions.

5. When you become angry with a peer, you:
___ A. Explode without giving it much thought.
___ B. Smooth things over with a good story.
___ C. Compensate for your anger by acting the opposite of your feelings.
___ D. Remove yourself from the situation.
___ E. Express your anger and invite a response.

6. When you find yourself disagreeing with other group members about a project, you:
___ A. Stand by your convictions and defend your position.
___ B. Appeal to the logic of the group in the hope of convincing a majority that you are right.
___ C. Go along with the group.
___ D. Do not participate in the discussion and don't feel bound by any decision reached.
___ E. Explore points of agreement and disagreement, then search for alternatives that take everyone's views into account.

7. When one group member takes a position in opposition to the rest of the group, you:
___ A. Point out publicly that the dissenting member is blocking the group and suggest that the group move on without her if necessary.
___ B. Make sure the dissenting member has a chance to communicate her objections so that a compromise can be reached.
___ C. Encourage members to set the conflict aside and go on to more agreeable items on the agenda.
___ D. Remain silent because it is best to avoid becoming involved.
___ E. Try to uncover why the dissenting member views the issue differently so that each member of the group can reevaluate her position.

2

8. When you see conflict emerging in your team, you:
    ___ A. Push for a quick decision to ensure that the task is completed.
    ___ B. Avoid outright confrontation by moving the discussion toward a middle ground.
    ___ C. Relieve the tension with humor.
    ___ D. Stay out of the conflict as long as it is of no concern to you.
    ___ E. Share with the group your impression of what is going on so that the nature of the impending conflict can be discussed.

9. In handling conflict between group members, you:
    ___ A. Anticipate areas of resistance and prepare responses to objections prior to open conflict.
    ___ B. Encourage your members to be prepared by identifying in advance areas of possible compromise.
    ___ C. Promote harmony on the grounds that the only real product of conflict is the destruction of friendly relations.
    ___ D. Submit the issue to an impartial arbitrator.
    ___ E. Recognize that conflict is healthy and press for the identification of shared concerns and/or goals.

10. In your view, one group might fail to work with another because:
    ___ A. There's a lack of a clearly stated position or a failure to back up the group's position.
    ___ B. There's a tendency for groups to force their leaders to abide by the group's decision, as opposed to promoting flexibility, which would facilitate compromise.
    ___ C. There's a lack of motivation on the part of one group's membership to live peacefully with the other group.
    ___ D. There's irresponsible behavior on the part of a group's leaders, resulting in the leaders' placing emphasis on maintaining their own power positions rather than addressing the issues involved.
    ___ E. There's a tendency for groups to enter negotiations with a win/lose perspective.

Now, add up your scores for each letter. For example, add up all numbers in the blanks in front of A completions, then do the same for all B completions. Repeat the process for C, D and E. Put the totals in the blanks on the next page. (Note: When you add your scores together for all five letters, their sum should be 120.)

Your next step is to transfer the scores to the chart that appears below.

Total As _____ Dominator

Total Bs _____ Compromiser

Total Cs _____ Placater

Total Ds _____ Withdrawer

Total Es _____ Collaborator

Finally, circle your highest score. That one is your dominant conflict management style. Put an asterisk (*) next to your second highest score. That's your secondary conflict management style and is important because it usually appears when you're feeling afraid or angry.

Now let's explore what each of these styles means.

Collaborator — The collaborator is someone who is willing to work through a conflict and look for a win-win solution.

Placater — The most important priority for the placater is to end the conflict and make the other person happy again. They do this by allowing the other person to have her own way in a conflict.

Dominator—The dominator is win/lose-oriented when dealing with conflict. The dominator always intends to be the one who wins.

Compromiser — Though a compromiser believes she is achieving a small win, the result is just the opposite: In a compromise both people feel equally unhappy since no one gets what was desired.

Withdrawer — When a withdrawer perceives she is going to lose, she prefers to simply remove herself from the situation.

> *"Everything I do is connected up with my past life ... from my mother's milk to this glass of beer, everything is connected up."*
> Langston Hughes

2

Understanding the Five Styles

Now let's look more carefully at these styles and see how to use each of them and when not to use them.

Collaborating

This is a conflict management style in which people are seeking an exchange of information. In this style there is a genuine desire to examine the differences and reach a solution that is acceptable to everyone. This style is usually associated with problem-solving. Collaboration is effective when issues are complex and conflict levels are low.

Positive aspects of this style:

1. The collaborating style encourages creative thinking. Developing alternatives is one important strength of this style.
2. Its emphasis on both self and others synthesizes information from differing points of view.
3. Collaboration is also good to use when the issue is too important for compromise and you don't want to lose any commitment or you don't want to negotiate the fundamental goals.
4. This style is excellent when the people and the problem are clearly separate. It is usually fruitless when people really want to fight.

Negatives of this style:

1. This is not an effective style when a party lacks commitment or when time is short, because collaborating is a lengthy process.
2. It also becomes a frustrating style during higher levels of conflict, because reason and rational considerations are often overshadowed by emotional commitments to a position.
3. Not all conflicts are worth the time and energy collaboration requires.

Collaboration is good to use when you need a high level of commitment from everyone involved. (If your team doesn't have a high level of "buy in" to your priorities, it would be helpful to examine your use of collaboration.)

> *"Patience is the best remedy for every trouble."*
> Plautus

36

When you want to use it you can say:
- "There seem to be different opinions here; let's get to the bottom of this."
- "Let's get several people from each work group together and discuss the options."
- "How can we all move to a satisfactory position on this?"

Note: 93 percent of us are collaborators when we take the previous test, but remember that we use our secondary style when we're under stress.

Exercise

Describe a problem or conflict that you solved through collaboration. (How) did a collaboration style help you?

_____

_____

_____

_____

Placating

Placating, or giving in, is another conflict management style. Like the other styles this is a legitimate and useful strategy. Here are four times when placating is useful:

1. Placating is useful when the need for harmony is high.
2. It is a good method for developing relationships and building up "credits" to use at another time when you have to resolve a more important issue.
3. Placating, used in non-critical situations, is a way to let your employees learn through mistakes.
4. Most of all, this method is useful when you realize that you are wrong.

Think about this: Placating places a high value on others but a low value on one's self. Sometimes it indicates low self-esteem. If people use it consistently, it can also mean that they have trouble admitting they are wrong.

This style gives power to others. When you choose to use it, you can say:

- "I don't care — do whatever you want."
- "You're the expert; what do you think?"

Exercise

In the space below, describe a situation in your workplace when placating would be a good method to use.

_____

_____

_____

_____

Which of the reasons that you chose placating applies to your situation?

_____

_____

Dominating

This is the style that's the opposite of placating. Here emphasis is placed on self. While the placating or obliging person may neglect her own needs, the dominating person overlooks the needs of others. This strategy can be reactionary or defensive. Dominating is associated with bullying and hardball tactics. It also is associated, sometimes positively, with decisive and deliberate leadership.

Here are four times to use this style:

1. When a decision needs to be made quickly. (There is no time to discuss or negotiate.)
2. When a matter is unimportant. (We're simply not going to spend time negotiating which brand of coffee to provide for the break room.)
3. When you have knowledge, you are right and the situation demands closure. (I just came from the warehouse, and they don't have the inventory to ship.)
4. When there is an unpopular change to be made that is important and in which there really is no room for discussion or compromise. (The new health insurance program is the only one management would approve.)

2

When the dominating style is used, someone always wins and usually someone loses. The dominator intends to be the person who wins. If this is your style, you tend to get things done and people look to you for a solution. However, you may burn some bridges along the way and will certainly leave others dissatisfied if this is your exclusive style.

The real positive aspect of a dominating style is to let people know something is not discussable. But if you always posture yourself with a dominating style, people will never know whether to negotiate and bargain. Use it carefully!

When you choose to use this style you might say:
- "I don't care — just do what I asked you to do."
- Or, "There are too many issues now — just save money."

Exercise

Describe when you have seen someone use this style appropriately.

_____

_____

_____

_____

Describe when you have seen someone use this style inappropriately.

_____

_____

_____

_____

Compromising

The compromising style is a middle-of-the-road style. It is neither high nor low in concern for others or for one's self. In compromise, everyone has something to give and something to take. It is ineffective when one side believes the other is wrong! It is powerful when both sides are right.

When to use it: Use compromise when other methods have failed and both parties are looking for a middle ground. Compromise may mean splitting the difference or exchanging concessions. Compromise almost always means each party gives up something. Using it means you may lose some commitment from everyone. In compromise you're looking for the small win, but it is not a true win, because both sides may still have unmet needs or unresolved issues.

This is an important clue. Once compromise is used effectively, close the door on this conflict by briefly discussing the unmet issues. If you do this, you'll see long-term results.

Compromise is best used when issues are not critical. It is a necessary tool when there's not enough time to work through collaboration. Compromise is a useful method to achieve temporary solutions until a permanent solution can be negotiated.

When compromise should be avoided:
- When either party is pushed by opinions or parties to the extreme, and they have nothing to give up.

- When you have a "big" party against a "little one," the public image of making the "little" guy give up is always poor.

- When another person must save face. The appearance of "giving in" that accompanies compromise often places an individual at an unfair resolution advantage.

Compromise as a deliberate strategy of conflict resolution is always driven by two factors:

1. What can I *not* afford to give up?
2. What is disposable in my thinking?

This attitude of asking for more than one wants or bluffing about one's resolve can easily become a counterproductive communication habit. Probably the best policy when using compromise is honesty, but caution should be taken ... not everyone will be honest during compromise.

2

Exercise

Describe a situation in your workplace when you used compromise.

_____

_____

What did you gain? _____

_____

What did you give up? _____

_____

Who looked like the winner? _____

_____

Who looked like the loser? _____

_____

Are there things you can do to get unresolved feelings of loss out in the open?

_____

_____

Withdrawing

This style is used by a "don't rock the boat" person. Using this method can mean issues never get resolved, because a major player withdraws from the situation. This can be frustrating to other team members.

When to use the withdrawer style: When issues are not important and not worth the cost of dealing with them, when more time is needed or when things need to "cool down." For example, during a meeting an issue can be "tabled" or postponed. Sometimes you might want to use the withdrawer style when you need to

collect your thoughts, gain control of your emotions or gather the data you need. Withdrawing is a helpful tactic to have in your toolbox, but, as with the others, avoid overuse.

When you need to use the withdrawer style, you can say:
- "Can we put this on hold temporarily?"
- "I haven't seen all the facts; I'll get back to you when ..."

Use this style to buy time, not to avoid problems. Be sure to follow up, or you may be left out of the decision. The withdrawer can slow down momentum of anger and conflict by saying, "We need some time out. Let's collect our facts, and regroup in 15 minutes." It also is an excellent strategy to employ when you are being pulled into a conversation — gossip — for example, that makes you uncomfortable. Here's a good exit line: "What you are talking about is really beyond my information at this time. I'll need to check out of the conversation, but if you need my input later, I'll try to get up to speed."

Exercise

Describe a time when you used the withdrawer style effectively:

_____

_____

_____

What did you gain? _____

_____

Did you sacrifice anything because of using this tactic? _____

_____

What will you do to reenter the issue, if you must? _____

_____

_____

Conclusion

Now, look again at your score on the earlier exercise. The high score indicates your dominant style.

However, the second highest score is equally important, because that's the one you'll use under stress or under pressure of conflict. You see, we generally "use up" our preferred style early in the conflict, and as time and emotion drag on, we cease to find our No. 1 style effective. That's when we default to our backup style.

Be aware of this, and when you find yourself slipping into this style automatically, STOP, check yourself and be sure you are choosing the style that is most appropriate. You should be familiar with the five styles of managing conflict and not only know your own tendencies but understand how and when to use a particular style when the situation calls for it. This requires an ability to separate your emotions from the event and then consciously select a deliberate conflict management tactic.

If you have big gaps in the totals of your scores, you have the potential for becoming locked into a style. Large gaps indicate distance between preference styles, and leaps must be made to change.

If your totals are close, it means you might jump from one style to another, not staying with one style long enough. When the tourist asked the New York street musician how to get to Carnegie Hall, he replied, "Young man, practice, practice, practice." This is also how you will become skilled at being able to use all of the conflict management styles ... practice, practice, practice.

Reflect on your boss's handling of a recent conflict. What style

> *"Conflict is not often seen as productive. Most people avoid it. In the process, they avoid clarity and progress."*
> Kaleel Jamison

2

Exercise

Reflect on a recent situation where you felt you could have handled conflict better.

What style did you use? _____

_____

Which style do you think would have been more successful? _____

_____

Why?_____

_____

was she using? Did it work? How would you analyze what could/should have been done? If you disagree with it, what would you do, based on what you've learned here? If you have trouble working with someone, step back from the conflict and assess her style. Knowing these five conflict management styles can save you a great deal of aggravation.

When you recognize a style and consider it inappropriate, simply say, "You're trying to get me to compromise, and I'm not ready to give up anything at this point," or "You're withdrawing unnecessarily; we need you in this discussion."

The Burger Method of Constructive Confrontation

Here is an easy-to-use technique for confronting inappropriate behavior. This technique is learned very easily, and it's one of the most useful skills you can have. It's called the "Burger Method" because it always uses three simple statements, like two pieces of the bun with meat in the middle.

Conflict can raise different points of view.

The three parts of the burger are:
Statement I: The Triggering Event
Statement II: Your Feeling(s)
Statement III: The Reason

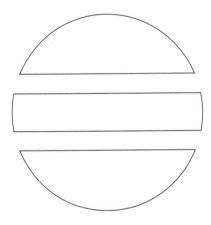

Example: Your secretary is consistently late for work.

You say:
- "Pat, when you come late for work (I),
- I feel frustrated (II)
- because I have to cover for you until you get here." (III)

Notice again, that first you analyze and describe what happened ("When you do this" or "When this happens"). Next, share your feelings about what happened, and finally, give the reason for your feelings.

45

This is followed by a statement or question such as, "Can we talk?" This question invites the other party to seek resolution of the problem.

Power is not bad unless it is wrongly used.

To use this method effectively, it is important to:

- Identify the triggering event. Describe as accurately as possible what the other party did.
- Identify and own your feelings. To own your feelings, say simply, "I feel." Never say, "You made me feel." Then explain the reason you feel as you do.
- Avoid blaming language such as, "You made me," "You should have," etc. This is putting the problem on the other person, and it will create greater conflict, not encourage resolution.

Here are three other examples of how to use the Burger Method:

1. *Situation:* You have not received the weekly customer orders as expected, and inventory control is slipping.

   Burger technique: "When the orders are not on my desk in time (I), I feel anxious (II) because I can't get the customers their inventory when promised (III)."

2. *Situation:* Printouts of your department's reports are needed so you can prepare for the upcoming staff meeting, and they're late.

   Burger technique: "When you don't have the printouts prepared (I), I get frustrated (II) because we can't have the information we need for the staff meeting (III)."

3. *Situation:* A team member has covered for you on many occasions; messages are left for you but you *never* get them.

   Burger technique: "When you don't give me my messages (I), I feel upset (II) because I discover a problem later and then get angry (III)."

Exercise

Now it's your turn. Think of two situations at work where you can use this "Burger Method," and write the three statements you would use for each:

1. Situation: _____

   When this happens: _____

   I feel: _____

   Because: _____

2. Situation: _____

   When this happens: _____

   I feel: _____

   Because: _____

3. Situation: _____

   When this happens: _____

   I feel: _____

   Because: _____

Types of Conflict

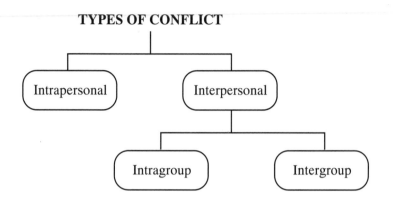

TYPES OF CONFLICT

Reprinted with permission from *How to Manage Conflict*, page 30, by Dr. William Hendricks, copyright 1991, National Press Publications, Overland Park, KS.

Rena and George are feeling frustrated because they've had to share an office during renovation and their work styles are different. George is very quiet and keeps his space neat, while Rena is an exuberant extrovert whose file system consists of various stacks of paper here and there. George was recently promoted and is not sure he is up to the new assignment. Lately he's not been sleeping well, and that doesn't help him cope with the office arrangement. Rena's marketing staff recently took on a new member who has very different ideas about how the work group should function and has voiced strong critical opinions about some of their previous work. George's team is functioning well, but the group is locked in battle with the computer services department.

"All your actions as a mediator are also demonstrations of good communication."
Kenneth Kaye

2

As with Rena and George, when you stop and think about it, there are several arenas in which you have conflict. Some conflict is within yourself. Some conflict is with other people. Conflict within yourself or some kind of inner struggle is called *intrapersonal* conflict. Conflict between people, *interpersonal* conflict, is the name assigned to describe what happens within groups or organizations. Both are important to understand, and both need to be handled.

Conflict within yourself or some kind of inner struggle is intrapersonal conflict.

Intrapersonal Conflict

When your expertise, your interests, your goals or your values are stretched beyond your comfort level, you experience internal distress. When this happens it hampers your day-to-day living and can become immobilizing.

When conflict is experienced internally it can stem from a physical, a mental or emotional cause. At its mildest level it produces symptoms such as headaches, backaches, etc. But when the next level of stress is reached, it causes "burnout" or, at its extreme, suicide.

How you deal with intrapersonal conflict will determine whether you can deal with interpersonal conflict effectively. The first step is to have control of the event externally, by asking the following questions to examine whether intrapersonal conflict is a current issue for you.

Interpersonal conflict describes what happens within groups or organizations.

1. Are there people you consistently avoid? Avoidance is a coping mechanism and usually signals low levels of conflict and stress.

2. Do you find yourself looking for some release from the day-to-day pressures of work? One school of pop psychology has taught that we can vent our feelings and emotions by redirecting the energy into other activities. This works for some. The important point is to be aware of your need to vent your feelings — it's another sign of intrapersonal conflict.

3. Do you find it nearly impossible to get out of a problem-solving mode even when you've left the office? If you care about an issue, you're more likely to experience stress over it. Intrapersonal conflict is one sign of your concern. An inability to "put things away" shows an internal seething common to those struggling with intrapersonal stress.

Don't despair if you answered "yes" to each of the questions above. Most middle managers do. Intrapersonal conflict can be used as a biological alert system that shows where energy is being drained away and where you need to focus your personal management skills. But you must learn to listen to your body:

- Know your blood pressure and cholesterol levels
- Know which aches and pains are justifiably "old age" and which ones signal stress and conflict
- Know whom to talk to about your concerns:
    1. Do you have people you trust who will listen attentively?
    2. Do you have an inner voice that picks you up when you are down? The power of self-talk can make a real difference.
    3. Do you know whom to go to when you need "cheering up" and when you need constructive criticism?
    4. Do you set aside pride and get professional help when you see that the conflict has escalated to an internal level too great to handle?

Interpersonal Conflict

There are two subgroups of interpersonal conflict: intragroup and intergroup. When a conflict occurs *within* a small specific group, it's called *intragroup conflict*. When many groups are involved in a conflict, it is classified as *intergroup conflict*.

For example, when the marketing and creative departments have a disagreement with each other, you have intergroup conflict: that's happening between departments.

"You don't want to waste time and money prolonging a situation that isn't going to get better. But you don't want to lose good people whose problems could have been solved."
Kenneth Kaye

Intergroup conflict, of course, is the most complex and the most serious to an organization, because there are more people and emotions involved. Any time conflict escalates and spreads among groups, the gossip and rumor mill operates and brings harm to you and your business. Have you experienced an intergroup conflict recently?

The tension between old and new team members within the same department or team is an example of intragroup conflict. It is best to address conflict when it involves only the smallest segment of people. Once two or more personalities become involved, it is likely to escalate and become more destructive and harmful.

An excellent first step in conflict management is to classify the event as interpersonal or intrapersonal and then identify what it is doing to you personally. If you know who is involved and whether the conflict has spread from a localized (focused) event to a broader-based conflict involving more people, you are less likely to be pulled uncontrollably by emotions or fears. You can always assume that an increase in involved people brings generalized problems that are less clearly defined and much more likely to require multiple solutions.

Exercise

Take a moment to review conflicts from your past, as well as intergroup and intragroup conflicts you have observed.

Intragroup: _____

_____

Intergroup: _____

_____

Now review the intrapersonal conflict you experienced during these conflicts. How did your body alert you or react to the event?

Identifying Conflict Stages

Picture a set of stair steps, each step ascending higher and higher than the previous. That's similar to how conflict can be viewed. You can think of conflict as a series of escalating steps that can be managed. This image will help you respond effectively and appropriately. Furthermore, as you analyze conflict, you see that not all conflicts are equal. They come not only in all sizes and shapes but at varying levels or stages. Identifying conflict before it escalates, at a low stage, and taking deliberate actions can turn a problem into an opportunity. However, if conflict is left unattended, it's dangerous to you and your organization.

> *"Problems are only opportunities in work clothes."*
> Henry J. Kaiser

Three Stages of Conflict

Stage One: Daily Events
Stage Two: Challenges
Stage Three: Battles

Three Stages of Conflict

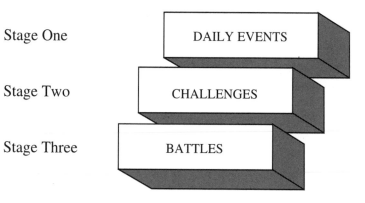

Stage One   DAILY EVENTS

Stage Two   CHALLENGES

Stage Three   BATTLES

Reprinted with permission from *How to Manage Conflict*, page 6, by Dr. William Hendricks, copyright 1991, National Press Publications, Overland Park, KS.

2

Stage One conflict is the least threatening and easiest to manage. As it escalates to Stages Two and Three, it becomes more difficult to manage and the potential for harm to you and others increases.

Conflict moves between stages but doesn't necessarily follow a linear pattern. If you discover a Stage One conflict at work in the morning and do nothing, by the end of the day it could well have escalated to Stage Three. The opposite is also possible: A high-level conflict will sometimes unexpectedly dissipate with time. So what are you to do? First, let's explore some underlying characteristics of conflict.

Characteristics of Conflict

1. *As conflict escalates, concern for oneself increases.* As conflict moves to higher stages, a person in conflict focuses on self-interest. The team is not important, the other person is not important, the company is not important. Self-preservation — whether it's physical, emotional or even ideological — is all that matters.

2. *The desire to win increases with a rise in self-interest.* Saving face takes on increased importance at higher levels of conflict. A person in higher levels of conflict says and does what it takes to make herself look good, including hiding out or covering things up.

3. *Nice people can become harmful to others as conflict increases.* It is surprising but predictable to see normally calm people lose their temper, go into a rage or attack others in the heat of conflict. Under pressure people shift, unconsciously, into their alternate style of handling conflict, which is usually less effective.

4. *Conflict management strategies that work at low levels of conflict are often ineffective and at times counterproductive at higher levels of conflict.* Perhaps you have been mildly upset at something and, when someone offers to help, you respond with appreciation. Another time, however, when you are extremely upset, the same offer may make you react

> *If you discover a Stage One conflict at work in the morning and do nothing, by the end of the day it could well have escalated to Stage Three. The opposite is also possible ... So what are you to do?*

angrily with something like, "Just leave me alone!" Collaboration at low levels of conflict is usually helpful and is often seen as a hindrance at high levels of conflict.

5. ***Conflict may skip levels.*** You don't always have the chance to handle a conflict at Stage Two if you ignore it at Stage One. Conflict and people are volatile and can blow up unexpectedly. At any one time, you may find an individual at all three levels, because her frame of reference keeps shifting.

6. ***People are likely to be at different levels during conflict, but an overall organizational level of conflict can be identified.*** Organizations have personalities and cultures. Sometimes a couple of people can have a negative effect on the whole organization. As a supervisor, if you manage the interpersonal conflicts, the organizational level will be managed as well.

Finding Solutions

A skinned knee doesn't call for major surgery, and a heart attack needs more than a Band-Aid. Likewise, the three levels of conflict require strategies appropriate to their intensity.

- A Stage One conflict and its accompanying emotions can best be addressed with coping strategies.
- Stage Two conflicts require more training and specific management skills.
- At Stage Three,' intervention is necessary and generally requires a neutral third party.

Coping with Low-Level Conflict

Characteristics of Stage One Conflict

Stage One conflicts are the daily irritations that come from living and working with others. Perhaps there is disagreement over who makes the coffee in the office, or who is on the memo routing list or how to keep the wait line at the copy machine from getting so long. You can easily think of examples from your own experience. These little annoyances accumulate throughout the day, each too small to pay attention to, but the inner emotion monitor, the interpersonal conflict meter, is usually running.

> *"Anger as soon is fed is dead, 'tis starving makes it fat."*
> Emily Dickinson

2

Although conflict at this stage is usually handled unconsciously, it is most effective when it's handled deliberately; otherwise an irritation can become a problem, and a problem can become a crisis. Why does this happen? Such a shift comes about because of the persons involved: different personalities, different coping mechanisms and ever-changing life events.

Using Avoidance and Obliging

Avoidance is a commonly used strategy for some Stage One irritations. Minor things can be passed off rather than dealt with. You use silence with your boss when you choose it as a tactic preferable to discussion. You avoid confronting a co-worker when you decide personal irritations are not worth mentioning. Perhaps your contact with the individual is minimal, so you take a "live and let live" attitude.

Exercise

Describe a situation when avoidance was the appropriate strategy for you to use:

_____

_____

_____

Why was it right for you? _____

_____

_____

Obliging is a slightly stronger version of avoidance. It is when an individual "gives in" to another. This involves a person's desire to "fit in" and belong. It usually overrides lower levels of conflict. Deliberate obliging can be beneficial to team effort, but there is no way to predict how long an individual will oblige.

2

C A S E   S T U D Y

Example:

> Roger's team decides to change the time of its regular Monday meeting. Everyone except Janet wants to meet at 9 a.m. Janet obliges and goes along, though unhappily. It's possible that Janet may settle comfortably into the new time, but at some point she could revert to passive/aggressive behavior by being silent or sullen or perhaps deliberately late. At some point during the meeting, she may overreact because of her frustration over this earlier issue.

As you can see above, avoiding or obliging can backfire on you or a group. It's not necessarily the best option. You must weigh the consequences and consider your options carefully. Don't get caught reacting to conflict without an intentional commitment to the style you use.

Must you have a constant conflict monitor running in your brain? Must you calculate every response? At Stage One, probably not, but you'd best be alert and ready when the conflict hits Stage Two or Three.

Collaboration — The Preferred Conflict Style at Stage One

The most satisfying and effective style of conflict management at Stage One is collaboration. The win-win spirit that is generated through this style allows people to go about their jobs with positive and constructive relationships while handling the daily irritations.

Collaboration requires a sense of detached discussion. Collaboration requires a setting where people are not overly invested in one point of view or one perspective. Collaboration is effective when people can step back from an issue, separate the emotion from an issue and discuss options that are mutually beneficial, which is usually possible at Stage One, because people are less invested and the conflict is fairly localized.

The secret to being an excellent conflict manager is to capture the Stage One conflict and turn it into a collaborative discussion. As your people learn it's acceptable to have differing opinions and respect for each other. This open and honest atmosphere creates opportunity for problems to be discussed before they ever escalate.

As a manager, your job is to monitor when a day-to-day irritation becomes a problem so you can deal with it out in the open.

Stage One Characteristics
1. At Stage One, parties feel discomfort and possibly anger but are quick to "pass off" these emotions.

2. Individuals are usually willing to work toward a solution with a sense of optimism that "we can work this out" or "this is no big deal."

3. Facts and opinions are shared openly with one another once the problem has surfaced.

4. Communication is usually clear, specific and oriented to the present because the people and the problem are not as intertwined as they are in more intense conflict.

How to Handle Stage One Conflict (Coping Strategies)
1. Initiate creative problem-solving using a process that examines both sides of the issue. Keep everyone looking at both sides; communicate openly.

2. Brainstorm together. This works well because you can discuss problems and not personalities. Remind people that there are no bad ideas in brainstorming, so everyone finds a point of comfort.

3. Evaluate the brainstorming by asking lots of "What if" questions.

4. Ask whether the reaction (conflict) is in proportion to the situation. Are there residual emotions carrying over from another disagreement? This tactic can really clean out the skeletons in the closet. If done well, you can expunge the past record of many team members.

5. Identify points of agreement and work from these points. Only then identify points of disagreement. Help all sides

> *The person not on the defensive is in control.*

see the big picture. Understanding alone will often dissolve Stage One conflicts. People need to know they are being heard.

6. Spend time making sure everyone is part of the conflict resolution process.

Remember it is much easier to handle these conflicts at this level than at higher stages. You have the most control at this level.

Managing Stage Two Conflict

Characteristics of Stage Two Conflict

1. Competition enters the conflict at the second stage. People adopt a "win-lose" attitude and become competitive. At this stage "how one looks" and a "cover your hind end" attitude are joined with keeping score of one's verbal victories.

2. The people and the problem become intertwined, and the level of commitment needed to work through the conflict also increases. Coping strategies such as avoidance and obliging must be replaced with people-managing strategies.

3. A lack of trust makes people less likely to be accurate with facts. Furthermore, the nature of the dialogue changes and becomes less specific. You'll hear generalizations such as "they" and "everyone believes" as well as words like "always" and "never."

4   While the atmosphere isn't necessarily hostile at Stage Two, it is cautious, and put-downs or sarcasm are frequently used.

How to Handle Stage Two Conflict (Managing)

As a manager you must *separate the people from the problem* as a first step to managing Stage Two conflict. Here are some ideas:

1. Create a safe atmosphere. Provide an environment where everyone is secure in feeling their needs will be met:

<hr>

Who's "they"?

- Make the setting informal. It is helpful to sit in a circle, which is less competitive than sitting across a table.
- Establish neutral turf.
- Have an agenda.
- Be in control.
- Set the tone. As the discussion leader, be slightly vulnerable.

2. Be hard on the facts, soft on the people. Clarify generalizations. Insist on specifics. Who is "they"? Is "always" an accurate description?

3. Work as a team. Share the responsibility for finding an acceptable alternative. Don't carry this load for the group! Use the words "we," "us" and "our" as you describe problems and concerns.

4. Look for middle ground, but don't suggest compromise. Compromise is perceived as losing important points. Instead, creatively look for the middle ground by focusing on the points of agreement.

5. Don't rush. Don't push for closure. Defusing the emotional tension of conflict takes time, as does allowing the parties involved to find acceptable solutions. Take some time to let emotions flush out, or you'll visit them again later.

Working with Stage Two Conflict

At Stage Two it's important to realize that facts are slanted and winning is important to all parties involved. The suggestion that we compromise is exactly what is needed but will be most resisted. The real secret is to "buy" some time, but do everything you can to keep the major players away from outside contingencies. Here's what often happens during a Stage Two discussion if a resolution is not identified and the meeting breaks up to be continued at a later time …

Bob says to his peers, "That was a waste of time. Shelly doesn't have a clue of what's important, and I told them what I thought. You should have seen them squirm over the real facts. Not one person in the room challenged me. We've got them on the ropes over this issue — it's only a matter of time."

C
A
S
E

S
T
U
D
Y

Shelly says to her peers, "That Bob's a real jerk! He didn't listen, and he still doesn't have a clue about what's really happening. But I told them all the truth. We couldn't solve it yet, but we will. It's just a matter of time before they give in. Trust me, I can get us what we need."

Do you see what's happening? Bob and Shelly are still competing and trying to marshal their army for support, and now even if an acceptable middle ground is found, they must "look good" to their peers or they've failed. Stage Two becomes a very sticky set of dynamics.

Compromise is the right approach, but move toward it cautiously. Here are some suggestions:

> *"If you argue and rankle and contradict, you may achieve a temporary victory — sometimes; but it will be an empty victory because you will never get your opponent's good will."*
> Benjamin Franklin

1. Very early in the discussion, create a verbal and sometimes written contract of common goals. Let everyone know the big picture that surrounds the issues. It is often important for one person to act as a leader and be fairly directive in getting this "big picture" identified.

2. Secure a commitment from each party. It is not acceptable to withdraw or quit. Affirm the fact that every person and every perspective is needed. Again, it's important to create this verbal agenda, and it does not emerge unless someone is fairly directive. Make sure you can affirm several strengths of each person, and don't be afraid to mention them early in this discussion.

3. Create a set of ground rules and pre-call points of contention up front. For example: "We've got some real serious problems that are affecting our department. I'd like to suggest some ground rules for finding a solution to our problems. Please read over these, and then we can add to or modify them to meet our needs."
    *   Everyone has a right to their opinions and will be expected to share them.
    *   Some of us are angry, but we will not attack each other.
    *   It is important for each of us to "win," but let's make sure the company becomes the big winner when we are through.

2

- Discussion outside this meeting will only escalate the issues. If asked, simply say, "Things are progressing. I'll let you know when I have a good answer."
- We will always separate the person from the problem. If there are personnel concerns, we will address them once we have a solution to the problem.

As you can see, Stage Two requires work and a deliberate approach. It is the role of the manager to manage when conflict hits Stage Two. You must take charge at Stage Two or you'll have a war at Stage Three.

Intervention — Handling High-Level Conflict

Characteristics of Stage Three Conflict
When conflicts reach Stage Three, the parties involved no longer want to win but want to hurt or get rid of the other side. Being right and punishing the wrong become the consuming motivations.

At Stage Three, factions develop, sides are chosen and "the good of the organization" is equated with "our position." Even after the dispute is settled, some people will continue their fight as if they were on a "holy mission."

At this very serious stage, a nonpartisan third party must be brought in. You don't necessarily need a professional, but you do need someone who will be respected by all parties and someone who will be perceived as impartial. Depending on what's at risk, outside help is not a bad option.

It should be obvious that you want to deal with conflicts at Stage One and avoid Stage Three. Is it possible to move backward and de-escalate the conflict? Yes, but only if you determine where you are, remove barriers and rebuild trust. And rebuilding trust is not easy.

> *It is the role of the manager to manage when conflict hits Stage Two. You must take charge at Stage Two or you'll have a war at Stage Three.*

Working with Stage Three Conflict

By now, you should have a pretty clear sense that you are in deep trouble. At Stage Three all the rules of human courtesy disappear, and each party's loss of perspective is clear to an outsider. Often the words that are spoken don't match the actions and attitudes. For example:

> Ralph says angrily, " I really respect Joe, but he's dead wrong, and I'm not going to even try until he gets his act together." Stage Three translation — get rid of Joe and I'll try.

> Mary says, "Everyone involved must apologize to me, and then we'll discuss what should be done." Stage Three translation — There's only my perspective, and I expect everyone to give in to me.

How to Handle Stage Three Conflict (Intervening)

Conflict management styles are severely limited in their effectiveness at Stage Three. If you withdraw, you may be shot on the way out the door! Speaking up may mean isolation from the "in crowd." As factions form, every participant must be alerted to the realities of this issue and the severity of continuing on this course. Here are some major guidelines that must be followed:

1. Deal with the power. Refuse to allow spokespersons to act as translators. Get the real parties in the room.

2. Count the costs. Everyone should know what the extended logic of their position means. Who do we lose? Where are we now vulnerable? Stage Three always means loss, and it's advisable to know where you have the most and the least to gain.

3. Change is a fact. Once conflict has reached this point, everyone will be affected and things will be different. Anyone who thinks things can return to normal is wrong! Stage Three will help identify a new direction and a new course that is either destructive or constructive.

4. If major stakeholders exist, get them involved. If this conflict creates the situation of "Do this or lose the business," then there's only one choice. Don't let the minor players determine a major decision.

5. Create the expectation that once decisions are made, for either side, that everyone buys in or leaves. And immediately establish a course of action. Identify the big picture and then expect everyone to act in accordance with that vision.

6. Give people time to heal, but allow no further conflict on the issues. Shut the door behind you, or the argument will surface in a new form. Don't downplay the pain, but heighten the element of new possibilities. And keep the exit door open: "If you can't play our way, leave."

7. Find every opportunity to create cross-functional tasks. Put people together working on "new stuff" so they can set aside the old. Make it possible for people to identify new shared territory by giving them common goals and shared deadlines. Create an expectation of cooperation by assigning cooperative work.

Don't let the minor players determine a major decision.

Put people together working on "new stuff" so they can set aside the old.

63

2

Conflict Assessment Checklist

How do you know what level a conflict in your workplace has reached? Using the following questions, you can determine that in a matter of minutes. Try it now by thinking of a specific conflict situation as you go through the following questions.

STAGE ONE	YES	NO
1. Are individuals willing to meet and discuss facts?	[ ]	[ ]
2. Is there a sense of optimism?	[ ]	[ ]
3. Is there a cooperative spirit?	[ ]	[ ]
4. Does a "live and let live" attitude typify the atmosphere?	[ ]	[ ]
5. Can individuals discuss issues without involving personalities?	[ ]	[ ]
6. Are the parties able to stay in the present tense?	[ ]	[ ]
7. Is the language specific?	[ ]	[ ]
8. Do solutions dominate the management efforts?	[ ]	[ ]

STAGE TWO		
1. Is there a competitive attitude?	[ ]	[ ]
2. Is there an emphasis on winners and losers?	[ ]	[ ]
3. Is it hard to talk about problems without including people?	[ ]	[ ]
4. Is the language generalized?	[ ]	[ ]
5. Can you identify these statements?		
"They are/Everyone is ..."	[ ]	[ ]
"You always ..."	[ ]	[ ]
"He never ..."	[ ]	[ ]
6. Is there a cautious nature when issues are discussed?	[ ]	[ ]
7. Can you detect a "cover your hind end" attitude?	[ ]	[ ]
8. Do parties make efforts to look good?	[ ]	[ ]

STAGE THREE		
1. Are attempts being made to get rid of others?	[ ]	[ ]
2. Is there an intention to hurt?	[ ]	[ ]
3. Have obvious leaders or spokespersons emerged?	[ ]	[ ]
4. Is there a choosing up of sides?	[ ]	[ ]
5. Has corporate good become identified with a set of special interests?	[ ]	[ ]
6. Is there a sense of "holy mission" on the part of certain parties?	[ ]	[ ]
7. Is there a sense that things will never stop?	[ ]	[ ]
8. Has there been a loss of middle ground, allowing only black or white options?	[ ]	[ ]

2

Scoring Your Results ...

Let's take a look at the results. If you have more "yeses" than "nos" in the Stage One section, then you are likely facing a Stage One conflict. Your best course of action is to get the issues on the table fast. You have a full arsenal of conflict management styles that are appropriate at this stage. Select the best one for you and move forward.

Before you proceed, look at your "yes" and "no" scores in the Stage Two section. Although you are in a Stage One conflict, you may well also be in Stage Two, and you must always deal with conflict at its highest stage to be effective. More "yeses" than "nos" in the second section of the checklist is an indication of Stage Two conflict. It's time to be strategic and manage the problem. But before you act, check out the last section.

Count the "yeses" and "nos" in the last section of the checklist, and see if your conflict has escalated into Stage Three. If it has, walk gently and quickly assess who will be hurt by this problem, and identify your best outside source for intervention.

Commonly Asked Questions

Q. What if I have more "yeses" than "nos" in all three sections?
A. The likelihood is that your conflict has escalated to Stage Three. Deal with it as if it's a Stage Three conflict.

Q. Is it possible for people to be at more than one level?
A. Not only is it possible, it's probable! In fact, you will discover a full spectrum of stages. You must do two things:
   1. Identify the predominant stage and address the problem from that standpoint.
   2. Handle the highest levels of conflict first. If you don't, you'll get off track.

Q. Is it possible for problems to just go away?
A. Yes. It's also possible that it will snow in May, but don't count on it. When you start wishing for things to happen rather than making things happen, you've neglected your leadership responsibilities.

> *"Mediators have to be well acquainted with the biases and opinions of each party involved. They must be patient, understanding and neutral enough to be trusted by both sides."*
> Jimmy Carter

Q. Is there a foolproof way to get out of this mess, especially when it's at Stage Three?

A. Yes, but you must take control. It's always more uncomfortable waiting to do something than doing something. We usually get frozen in our reactions out of fear. Identify the worst-case scenario, adjust your strategy and act.

Q. My conflicts all come out in Stage Three. Is that common?

A. If you are personally stuck in Stage Three, then every problem looks exaggerated and threatening. De-escalate yourself or you'll carry baggage from all your conflicts into the others.

Q. What percentage of conflict is really Stage Three?

A. It's important to remember that, for some people, even Stage One conflict feels as if it's Stage Three. In addition, if unresolved conflict is sitting around in your experiences, that will affect the present problems. But in truth, most organizational conflict is Stage Two. Any good manager will act and stop conflict before it escalates to Stage Three. And all managers should act and resolve Stage Three the minute they see it!

The wise manager remembers:

1. **Frequently, conflict in business is at Stage Three. Stage Three resolution requires a high level of skill. Most people need help to handle this process. A better scenario is to deal with conflict when it is at Stage One and you can manage it.**

   When conflict escalates to Stage Three, it becomes very costly in time, money, morale and personnel fallout. A neutral team has to be trained or hired to deal with the conflict. Money and time are spent on the conflict instead of the team's work. If an outside team is used, valuable employee time is spent in interviews. Furthermore, informal gossip and discussion time is spent on the event, taking away from work. When the work force is polarized, inevitably morale suffers. When a Stage Three Conflict ends, there is the additional cost of money and time for personnel who may have to leave.

2. **Most people don't step in and manage conflict; instead they simply let conflict play itself out. The wise manager intervenes early and handles it at Stage One or brings it back down to where she can manage it.**

For some people, even Stage One conflict feels as if it's Stage Three.

66

2

Letting conflict play itself out is like playing Russian roulette with the odds stacked against you. Taking a passive rather than proactive stance may, in the short run, fool you into thinking it is the wiser course; however, there is almost always a much higher price to pay when the coals of conflict fan from a glow to a raging fire. Removing the hottest coals and dealing with those that can be handled is the first step at any stage.

3. **If the conflict is not resolved, it may seem to disappear on its own, but when the next conflict occurs, it will emerge not necessarily at Stage One but at the last highest stage.**

Although conflict may seem to die down, often it just "goes underground" until patience runs thin again or another event sparks things. That is when what might be a fairly trivial conflict suddenly becomes a serious conflict. The old conflict didn't really go away and the new conflict picks up at the intensity level of the previous one.

> Morris and George have been at odds for weeks over sharing equipment at the office. One of them gets frustrated now and then, but it usually seems to pass. After weeks of this, their manager calls a meeting to discuss reconfiguring the floor plan. She is blindsided when the question of their equipment comes up and they begin shouting at each other. This festering low-level conflict has escalated beyond Stage One.

*C
A
S
E

S
T
U
D
Y*

4. **Because there is so much conflict going on in our lives, resolution is never completed; resolution is always needed.**

We can never be rid of conflict. It is here to stay. Most people deal with multiple conflicts at any given moment. The more we develop our "conflict antennae" and deal with it pro-actively, the more skilled we become in handling conflict and anger and minimizing their negative effect on our lives.

Questions for Personal Development

1. What is the major emphasis of this chapter?

_____

_____

_____

_____

2. What are the most important things you learned from this chapter?

_____

_____

_____

_____

3. How can you apply what you learned to your current job?

_____

_____

_____

_____

4. How will you go about making these improvements?

_____

_____

_____

_____

5. How can you monitor improvement?

_____

_____

_____

_____

6. Summarize the changes you expect to see in yourself one year from now.

_____

_____

_____

_____

CHAPTER 3

Managing Differences

As you practice the skills you developed in the previous chapters, you're now dealing with the people you supervise in a way that's quite different from how the workplace has operated in the past. Managers today find they are more successful when they operate in a cooperative rather than in an adversarial manner, when they help people learn to get along better with each other and when they enable their staff members to be more self-directed and self-motivated. Conflict management and the self-empowering strategies we discussed provide an excellent venue for mentoring and building your people.

You know, however, that some workers still fight among themselves and that power plays still occur. In this section you'll learn six problem-solving rules and four keys to help eliminate in-fighting and to develop the kinds of relationships that make for a happier and more productive work environment.

> *"Avoid argument, but when a negative attitude is expressed, counter with a positive and optimistic opinion."*
> Norman Vincent Peale

Six Problem-Solving Rules

1. Attack the problem, not the person.
2. Describe (verbalize) your feelings, but never act on them.
3. Move from justification to resolution.
4. Look forward (to opportunity), not backward (by blaming).
5. Identify the points where you can give rather than take.
6. The angrier the event, the less likely logic will work.

Rule Number One: Attack the problem, not the person

Perhaps you've had the experience of coming upon a parent and young child in a public place. The child has misbehaved in some way, and the parent is unhappy about it. However, instead of correcting the behavior, he scolds the child by saying, "You're a bad, bad boy!" In your workplace you might hear two people arguing, with one shouting at the other, "You're a liar!" Or "You're just lazy and that's why you're not productive."

In each of these situations someone is failing to distinguish between the behavior and the person. This is not only counterproductive, it is destructive!

If you want a problem to be solved, it is essential to separate the behavior from the person.

If you want effective communication, if you want behavior to be changed, if you want a problem to be solved, it is essential to separate the behavior from the person. Whenever you have a problem with someone, you want to address the particular behavior, not that individual's personality.

It would be far better for the parent to say, "I do not like it when you scream in the store. If you can't speak in a quiet voice, we will leave." It would be more effective for the worker at the top of this page to say, "What you're saying doesn't match the information I have. Let's take another look at it." And in the other situation, "You're capable of higher output than this."

Attacking a person's character is never going to get him to change his behavior or attitude. It will simply make him more defensive. When we're defensive we can't be open to hearing about the need to change.

Attacking a person's character is never going to get him to change his behavior or attitude.

Rule Number Two: Describe (verbalize) your feelings, but never act on them

There's a big difference between describing your feelings and acting them out. For example, when you lose your temper, scream or name-call, you're expressing your anger or frustration. When you say, "I'm upset because your work was late," you're describing your feelings.

Which is more likely to get the result you want? The answer is obvious. But the question is "Why?" We know that when we have strong feelings we want to express them. When done in a healthy and successful way — for example, "I'm disappointed in the way you handled that" — you are releasing your feelings in a way that is constructive. On the other hand, if you let your feelings smolder and churn inside, you're more likely to release them in a form that will tear down rather than build up the possibility of getting good results.

Defining your feelings as well as the specific problem — "I'm upset because the other departments weren't notified in time" — shows that you are taking responsibility for your feelings. Furthermore, it names the specific behavior so the person is clear about what is upsetting you. In addition, when you make it clear you're offering your perspective and not making a character judgment, the other person is free to offer his, too.

All of this encourages open discussion and reduces defensiveness. *The less defensive everyone is, the more likely it is that the problem will get solved.* This is a simple but important rule. It's not hard but it takes practice, especially if you've had years of communicating the other way!

Rule Number Three: Move from justification to resolution
When something goes wrong, some people get stuck justifying their position and defending themselves. They are afraid to give up any ground. When a problem arises and your employee begins to explain, excuse or justify his behavior, move him quickly off that path to defining the problem and how to solve it. You'll be amazed at how surprised some of them are that you're not looking to place blame — and how gladly they'll join you in the "solution hunt."

> *"Understanding our task as conflict management rather than conflict resolution is a paradigm shift."*
> Roger Fisher

3

71

Rule Number Four: Look forward (to opportunity), not backward (by blaming)

When the building we're in catches fire, the important thing is to get everyone outside, not to stand around deciding who must be the arsonist. At work, do we want to find solutions to the problems and seize the opportunity, or do we want to spend time looking for a scapegoat? It makes much more sense to move forward to solving the problem. As a manager you can quickly discourage the tendency of others to place blame by ignoring those types of comments and redirecting the focus of the conversation to solutions.

A good rule is: no finger pointing, only solution pointing.

The gift that is wrapped inside of each problem is the opportunity to grow and learn. Life is too short to waste it making the same mistakes over again! If you get stuck on blaming, you'll get stuck in the past and repeat your mistakes because you failed to learn and grow.

There is something about human nature that instinctively wants to blame. In the story of the Garden of Eden, Adam pointed at Eve and said, "She made me do it." In the workplace, think how often you hear blame passed on to her, him, them, the company, the full moon, the government, parents or anyone else. The mature manager, dedicated to his own growth and development, will always look to take stock of the situation, to size up his responsibility for problems and learn what to do the next time to avoid failure.

Rule Number Five: Identify the points where you can give rather than take

Conflict resolution is a mutual process. You've got to be able to give when in a conflict. No situation that ends with win/lose results in a strong relationship afterwards.

So, when you go into a conflict resolution meeting, always have written out a list of concrete subjects to be discussed. In your own mind, be clear in advance about what you can live with or do without. Have an order of importance for your concessions in advance. Systematically tackle one point at a time until that point is agreed on to mutual satisfaction — or, if not resolved, at least agree to table it.

> *When the building we're in catches fire, the important thing is to get everyone outside, not to stand around deciding who must be the arsonist.*

> *A good rule is: no finger pointing, only solution pointing.*

72

Don't be like the woman who believes in fidelity but overlooks her fiancé's indiscretions in order to get to the altar and then is disappointed, angry and miserable later. Under no circumstances should you give away what is essential to you. To do this, you have to be clear about your bottom line.

Also be prepared to give something. Be ready to say, "I can postpone the project until the next fiscal year but not beyond," or "I don't want to lose this worker, but I will put him on loan to the other department for six weeks." Be clear about where you stand, what is negotiable and what is non-negotiable. This is how win-win situations can occur in conflicts.

3

Exercise

Take a few minutes now to think about a conflict you're dealing with or have dealt with recently.

Describe how you perceive the conflict:

_____

_____

_____

What is your bottom line on the issue?

_____

_____

_____

What are you willing to give on? (Rank items in their order of importance to you.)

_____

_____

_____

Rule Number Six: The angrier the event, the less likely logic will work

Your common sense and your experience tell you that the more things heat up in a conflict, the more likely people are to stop listening. Anger breeds defensiveness, and defensive people don't listen.

For your part, do everything you can to stay open, adaptable and friendly. Don't say or do things that make the other person defensive, and try not to let him make you defensive. Remember, it's hard for anyone to resist kind, nurturing language. Such language seldom goes in one ear and out the other. Have you ever been angry at someone and had them take the wind out of your sails by being sincerely caring? It's usually irresistible.

What if that fails? If things do heat up, your job is to stay calm and to diplomatically bring the topic back to the issue you're discussing. If that fails, call for a timeout, agree to put the issue on hold and arrange to meet another day. Don't immediately launch a counterattack.

Using these six rules for problem-solving, you'll never win an argument, but you will win plenty of agreement. That means you'll succeed at reaching your goal!

Four Keys to Being a Superior Supervisor

In this section there are four keys to help you implement the problem-solving rules previously discussed. These keys are aimed especially at building and strengthening the kinds of relationships with your staff that will encourage good problem-solving.

Key #1: If you want people to share their fears, recognize and talk about your own.
One of the best ways to improve your ability to manage people is to help them see that you have similar fears, hopes and goals. That's what this rule is about. No one can relate to a robot. No one can have a relationship with someone who never discloses his own feelings and fears. One of the first steps in building a team is establishing relationships that will help bridge the inevitable disagreements that occur. This key will help you lay the foundation for these types of relationships.

> *"Two heads are better than one only if they contain different opinions."*
> Kenneth Kaye

3

If you're new at this, pick areas of vulnerability you can discuss most easily. A good idea is to launch a vulnerability point to one person and make sure you can handle it before you share it with the whole team.

Key #2: If you want people to speak up, demonstrate that you want to hear what they have to say.

The key here is *listening*. Show your staff you can listen, and they will speak up. Communication involves taking full responsibility for listening to what others are trying to communicate as well as taking responsibility for sending clear messages. Listening is equally as — if not more — important than talking.

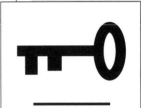

As you become adept at using these first two keys, you will build trust with those you supervise. Trust is the glue that holds a team together. Trust allows conflict to happen in a productive and non-destructive way.

Which of the first two keys needs to be used to build greater trust?

_____

_____

Key #3: If you want people to stop making negative assumptions, eliminate those assumptions in yourself.

People learn by modeling. Imitation is a conscious process, but modeling takes place unconsciously. In modeling, one person gradually takes on characteristics of another. If you walk around grouchy all day, how do you think your workers are going to act? If you have a pessimistic attitude, they will also. Whatever you give out is what you get back. In any organization, if the boss has a bad attitude, so will the workers.

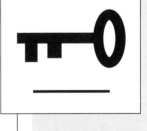

Parents are aware of this key. Probably every parent has caught himself at some time doing or saying exactly what his own parents did that he swore he'd never do or say. Whether a parent complains or brags about something he sees his child doing, it's probably appropriate to observe, "She doesn't get it from the wind." Sometimes it's a joy; sometimes it makes us cringe.

Firings will continue until morale improves!

3

We've all adopted some habits unconsciously. Examine your own behavior for being positive and for modeling this attitude to your staff.

Key #4: If you want people to ask questions about fear and anger, ask those questions first.

The best way to deal with fear is to face it and deal with it. As a supervisor you will find it liberating to approach fear directly, and you can be enormously helpful to your staff members by helping them learn to do the same.

When you have someone on your staff who is afraid, one of the most helpful things you can do is ask him to imagine what is the worst thing that could happen if his fear is realized. Once the worst is exposed, it can be countered and it's not as scary as he thinks.

Most people are not afraid of failure but of how they'd react in the face of it. They aren't sure they could handle it. Failing means losing control and being embarrassed. Few people look forward to that or know how they would handle it. Assurance may help them take the risk. What they learn is to handle risk and manage the fear associated with failure.

Knowledge and action are the greatest fear-busters. Learn about whatever it is that you fear. Face it by carrying out what you're afraid of. You'll be freed of that fear and empowered for other challenges!

Take a moment to examine your fears. What is something you are fearful of? How can you learn about it and face it? Who can help you with this?

After reviewing the four keys to being a superior supervisor and the six problem-solving rules, choose the four areas that you feel you need the most work, the four in which you are weakest. Are you quick to attack another person, ignoring the actual problem? Are you unable to verbalize your feelings of anger and fear? Do you move away from your fears rather than face them? Then write a brief assessment of where you are in those areas, where you'd like to be, and who or what will help move you ahead with it.

> *"If I never try anything, I never learn anything.*
>
> *If I never take a risk, I stay where I am.*
>
> *If I go ahead and do it, that affects how much I continue wanting to do it.*
>
> *But when I hold myself back, I trade appearances for the opportunity to find out what I am really like."*
> Robert Frost

Exercise

Area #1: Recognizing and talking about my fears

Where I am:

_____

Where I'd like to be:

_____

Who/what will help me move ahead with this:

_____

Area #2: Listening skills

Where I am:

_____

Where I'd like to be:

_____

Who/what will help me move ahead with this:

_____

Area #3: Modeling skills

Where I am:

_____

Where I'd like to be:

_____

Who/what will help me move ahead with this:

_____

Area #4: Dealing with fear

Where I am:

_____

Where I'd like to be:

_____

Who/what will help me move ahead with this:

_____

3

Negotiating a Solution

As you bring a conflict to a conclusion, you'll usually need to do some negotiating. In negotiating a solution, the question is how to get people to move from where they are to where you want them to be. You have tremendous power at this point because most people want to be out of the conflict and back on more productive tasks. Here are seven negotiating styles and the situations in which each works or doesn't work.

Negotiation is an integral part of conflict resolution. In the midst of conflict the best negotiators are able to put themselves in another person's shoes. Like the Native American prayer, "Oh Great Spirit, grant me the wisdom to walk a mile in another's moccasins before I judge him," the key to the art of negotiating is being able to stand in the other person's shoes and to understand what the situation is like for him. When you're familiar and comfortable with these seven styles of negotiating, you can adopt the one most appropriate for each conflict you face.

Style #1: Denial — choose not to listen

When It Works: When you need to separate yourself from the situation; when you need to buy time.

In this particular negotiating style, you choose to stop listening. When you use denial, your body is present but, in a sense, you've left the meeting. When you do this you give yourself the chance to think, to calm down or to take time. It may be that you've become so agitated you fear you might say something you'll regret and you want time to calm down. You need to separate emotionally from the situation, so you back off and think of something else to help you calm down.

When It Doesn't Work: When you're negotiating with someone and he knows you have the information he needs and you drift off. You give the impression that you are a selfish, one-way communicator.

> *Win-win can become gain-gain.*

Examples:

"I don't know" or "I don't recall that right now."

"I don't think I've seen those facts."

"I'm sorry, I wasn't part of that decision, so I'll have to withhold opinion now."

Style #2: Withdrawal — physically leave

When It Works: When the other person must have your participation.

When It Doesn't Work: When you have a lot to lose; when you're right; when someone will decide for you in your absence.

Unlike denial, in which you stay in the meeting, here you physically get up and walk out. This strategy is good to use when you need more information or more time. But don't fake these reasons. Withdrawal works only if your presence is pivotal to the discussion. If you're not needed and you get up and walk out, the others might be glad you're gone. You lose the chance to give your input and risk a decision being made without you. Furthermore, never use this strategy if you're right. If you're right and you leave, you obviously have a lot to lose.

> *Studies indicate that when withdrawal actually occurs, it's by the person who has the most accurate perspective.*

Some interesting studies indicate that when withdrawal actually occurs, it's by the person who has the most accurate perspective.

Style #3: Placating — you give way to power

When It Works: When the other person requires status.

When It Doesn't Work: If you need a real solution.

When you use this particular strategy, you're allowing the other person to be in charge, even if you disagree. You simply give away power in the interest of making the other person more agreeable by recognizing or elevating his status.

Sometimes people have what is called a "Yes, but" boss, who asks what you think but no matter what you answer responds, "Yes, but that won't work." In this case, if you try to placate by suggesting he should make the decision himself, he may not have a solution. People who consistently criticize are often afraid of making a decision upon which they can be judged. So, this negotiating style doesn't work when you need a real solution.

Style #4: Suppression — don't say what you really want to say
When It Works: When your information is damaging; when you need more time.
When It Doesn't Work: When the other party already has the information you're holding back.

This strategy is commonly known as "biting your tongue." Suppression is used infrequently yet is very effective in many cases. The benefit of this strategy is that it allows you to get your thoughts organized. People often use this in their personal lives with relatives. They refrain from saying what they'd really like to say, to keep the peace. If what you want to say won't help the process, it's a good idea not to say it.

Suppression can also be used as "silent blackmail." You know facts or issues about another party in a meeting and you hold back — they're never sure what you might divulge. Suppression in this instance can be used positively or negatively, depending on your ethics and values.

Suppression doesn't work when the other parties already have the information you're holding back. In this case you'll get more accomplished by being open. Using this tactic with any information that you both already share will lead the other party to conclude you're trying to be secretive.

These last three negotiating styles — dominance, compromise and collaboration — are the most popular.

Style #5: Dominance — try to overpower
When It Works: When you hold the power; at high levels of conflict/stress; when decisive leadership is needed.
When It Doesn't Work: When others don't respect your abilities or power; when others expect to participate; when parties are weak and reluctant to offer their views.

Lecturing children is normally a form of dominance, and it works well with young children because they respect your power. Parents know that as their children grow into teenagers, this is no longer true. You might be able to make your young child do what you say, but not your teen! Dominance works only when the other party acknowledges that you have control.

> *"Silence is argument carried on by other means."*
> Henry Che Guevara

If you tell your employees to do something and they know there won't be any consequences if they don't, are they likely to do it? Not if they don't believe you have the power to make them or that you *won't* make them.

Style #6: Compromise — both parties identify possible solutions
When It Works: When both parties are right; when you're concerned about maintaining relationships.
When It Doesn't Work: When only one party is right; when you have nothing to give up; when people must save face.

If you're negotiating with someone and it's really important to keep the relationship open or when the relationship is in jeopardy, compromise is effective. It works especially when you need a quick solution and are willing to make trade-offs. In every compromise both parties give up something, and both go away equally unhappy.

Compromise is a uniquely U.S. custom. In all other major languages, compromise is considered a negative event, and even in the English language, to compromise my values, or to put someone in a compromising position, carries negative overtones. Many people in conflict choose a place to dig in their heels, because to compromise means to give up something of value.

To combat the feeling of losing something of value, negotiators sometimes use "up-the-ante" tactics — asking for the moon in hopes of getting the most possible. In turn, the other party "low-balls" a deal, hoping to avoid negotiating too high of a deal. Deception and maneuvering have given negotiating a very bad name and are uncomfortable for many people.

The easiest and most productive compromise strategy is to know what you really want, identify what the other party really wants and then seek the greatest area of mutual benefit. All else then becomes "give up" options.

To compromise effectively, you must know what you want; you must know what's expendable and you must know when you should walk away.

No one can negotiate effectively once he is straddling the fence and cannot say "no."

> *"How insignificant this will appear a twelve-month hence."*
> Samuel Johnson

3

Style #7: Collaboration — expand your horizons

When It Works: When you have time; when a good relationship exists.

When It Doesn't Work: When there's a conflict of interest or a lack of trust.

With collaboration you're looking for a win-win solution, and you are able to expand your thinking to include additional options for resolution. Collaboration is a time-intensive strategy, so if a quick solution is needed, collaboration is not practical. When you use collaboration, both parties are happy in the end.

Knowing these seven styles will expand your skills in dealing with conflict or anger. In any given negotiating situation, you will always use at least two of these. Sometimes you'll need to use all seven.

Here is a story that demonstrates the use of these styles ...

Before discussing a problem, ask each party to describe the issues from the opponent's viewpoint.

3

C A S E S T U D Y

You're seated on a plane that's coming in for a landing. Something goes wrong and your plane crashes and catches fire. All the passengers are still in their seats, but smoke and flames are everywhere. Which of the above styles should we use here?

How about denial? Saying, "I don't think there's anything wrong. We're still in the air" clearly is not the way to solve the problem.

What about withdrawal? Should you just say, "I'm leaving but you stay here"? That would work for you but not for anyone else.

How about using placating? You could say, "Who'd like to leave first? Oh, you're bigger — would you like to go?" This is hardly a realistic solution.

Is suppression appropriate to use here? "I want to let people know we're in danger, but that might upset them, so I won't say it." Of course not.

Would dominance be an appropriate style to use in this situation? Absolutely. It's an emergency, and somebody needs to take charge. "You, open the door! You, help people out! Everybody, move!"

Then there's compromise. Compromise could be a quick fix. To say, "I'll get everyone out if you go find help" may be a good way to handle things.

Would you want to use collaboration? Is this the time to sit and down and discuss what might be done? No, you need a quick, definitive response.

So you can see that each of these styles is good for certain situations but not for every situation. You're most effective when you can choose the most appropriate style for the particular situation you're in. Let's look at a simple system that will help you determine, even in the middle of a conflict, which style is best to use. This system is called the ACES system, and it's composed of four steps.

Think of it this way: In poker, if you're dealt four aces, you know you have a really great hand. That's what you have with the ACES method, a great hand. You have four great cards to play if you recognize their value. You've probably tried to play cards with someone who didn't know the rules or value of his hand. Well, many managers try to manage conflict never knowing the strength of their hands.

Let's look at your four aces ...

Three stonecutters were asked what they were doing. The first said he was chipping stones to make each just the right size. The second replied he was earning his wages. And the third said he was building a cathedral.

The Four Aces

The "A" in Aces: Assessment
Every person is dealt a hand, and he plays the cards he's given. In conflict, you are dealt four aces. Imagine looking at your cards and seeing those aces! In conflict, the ability to play a winning hand is as easy as the aces in your hand. Notice we said easy, not simple.

The first ace is assessment. No one can effectively address a problem or concern without a clear sense of perspective. You must be able to identify who has the cards and who doesn't. If you tip your own hand too soon, you may find yourself sidetracked by bluffs, or others may fold realizing they cannot play the conflict through. In either case, to effectively manage conflict, you must keep everyone involved by accurately assessing the intensity and involvement of all parties. Here are some assessment questions you must learn to ask yourself:

"Where is this conflict leading me?"
"What is likely to happen, positively and negatively?"
"How did we get here?"
"Who is involved?"
"Do I need help, support or additional resources?"
"What's at risk?"
"Are there likely to be big winners or big losers if this continues?"

The "C" in Aces: Control

A good card player is able to look into the eyes of the players and see beyond the surface, read the trends and accurately predict the way cards will fall. The second ace you play is control. Either you control the damage or it will control you! As this card is played, you make sure the points where you or others are likely to be hurt are managed. In any fire, there are some coals that burn red hot and others, often on the edges, that just don't give off much heat. Here are some basic questions you must answer to make sure you are dealing with the strongest hands and handling the right issues:

Make sure the points where you or others are likely to be hurt are managed.

"Where is there great emotion and intensity?"
"Who is out of control?"
"Where are things being exaggerated or distorted?"
"Are there parties or positions that must be dealt with before solutions can be searched for?"
"Where is the source of greatest impact?"

The "E" in Aces: Engagement

An effective conflict manager has the cards, but it's at this point in the resolution process that an effective conflict manager makes his move. There are only so many things that can be done and only so many places he can put his time. This card reminds each of us to play cautiously and engage at the right time and in the right way. Too much intensity, and we'll scare off others or escalate the wagers. Too little and we may end up with unresolved issues, people folding before we have a chance to really play our cards. After all, how many times do you get four aces? Here are some questions you must know the answer to as you engage others in conflict resolution:

"What is expendable?"
"Are things really focused on opportunity, not blame?"
"Who or what are the driving factors?"
"Who are the major stakeholders?"
"What resources are being consumed?"

The "S" in Aces: Solution

Too frequently people attempting to manage conflict jump to the solution without a clear sense of the first three aces. The last ace you play is a solution, based on your assessment, control and engagement answers. Because conflict involves escalated emotion, it is easy to jump at what first looks like an easy fix or a fast solution. By playing this card last, you've had a chance to see the bigger picture. Here are the questions you must ask to reach a solution:

"Where do the opportunities for movement exist?"
"What can I expect as resistance and support?"
"Can I create common ground rules?"
"Can I create a best-case and worst-case scenario for discussion?"
"Where can I find win-win positions?"

Let's look at two scenarios in which several styles are needed.

Scenario #1:

Mike is the supervisor of a busy production department in a flourishing company. In the past three years the company has grown so much that his department can't keep up with the product demand without additional staff and equipment. However, in a recent management meeting, Mike's boss, the executive vice president, made it clear that he's not in favor of adding additional resources at this time. Mike is feeling increased pressure, and his staff is getting stressed out. Mike needs to negotiate a solution that will allow his department and the company to succeed, given the increased demands on his staff.

**C
A
S
E

S
T
U
D
Y**

85

Assessment ...

In this situation Mike must first *assess,* getting a clear sense of where the conflict and anger are stemming from. The triggering event is rapid growth of the company. Who owns the problem? Mike has a problem with production. In addition, his people are waiting for him to take care of the situation. The conflict and anger clearly stem from trying to manage the burden of work and people by himself. His boss and his people have abandoned him!

Control ...

With this information, Mike moves on to the *control* step. He knows there will be a negative chain of events if he does nothing more. However, things can get better if he begins to control the feelings and emotions that surround him. At this point, Mike knows what's bothering him, but he has not yet clearly stopped the flow of negative emotions and the feelings of being powerless. Mike's ability to develop his job, his people and his company depends on a clear sense of control when things are getting him upset. Let's look at some hot spots:

1. The boss. Mike heard his boss say, "No additional resources," but is that really true? How many times have you heard statements made in a meeting that were broad generalizations and not meant for you specifically? Mike needs to control his feelings about the boss and the situation, at least until he's sure of the facts.

2. Production. Demand is high and times have been good. This should be a time of celebration. In order to control his negative feelings, perhaps Mike needs to look for a moment at the alternative to having too much work — no work! That usually starts to bring a new perspective.

3. His staff. If they are waiting, Mike might want to ask himself, "Have I given enough authority and responsibility to them to solve this problem?" Mike is not in this alone, and in order to control the feelings of being trapped and frustrated, Mike must get more people involved in sharing the problem. It is not just his concern.

> *"This is the foundation of success nine times out of 10 — having confidence in yourself and applying yourself with all your might to your work."*
> Thomas E. Wilson

Engagement ...

Once Mike has a clearer sense of the events and facts, he must engage himself and start to focus on some aspect of the problem. In this case, it's probably wise to go talk to his boss and make sure of the facts about "no additional resources." He also needs to pull his people or a problem-solving team together and share his problem. There may not be an answer yet, but everyone can become informed of his concern and begin to think of alternatives.

Solution ...

Given the limitations of this case, solutions seem to point toward innovation, overtime or dropped deadlines. It becomes the problem for Mike, his boss and staff to find the best alternatives. Rent equipment, contract work outside, hire temporary workers or possibly reengineer the workflow, accessing people from other areas. Mike needs the authority of his boss, the creativity of his staff and the commitment of everyone to solve this problem.

There may not be an answer yet, but everyone can become informed and begin to think of alternatives.

3

To work toward a *solution*, Mike needs to begin negotiating. Would **denial** work here? No, because Mike knows that if he does nothing, the situation will quickly get worse. Maybe he should **withdraw** and gather more information to present a better case to his boss. Withdrawing would be appropriate but only for the time it would take him to prepare a more effective case.

What about **placating**? Placating would be an excellent strategy. Mike doesn't want to confront his boss too strongly or sound too negative, because his boss could become defensive and rigid. Placating also gives his staff room to complain and join the concerns. By not dominating with anger, Mike can move quickly to some form of compromise with his boss, his people or his product demands.

Compromise would be effective, because what Mike needs is quick alternatives to a pressing problem. However, **collaboration** is precisely what Mike must have. So, Mike's best scenario is to begin with *withdrawal* and move from *placating* to *collaboration*.

*C
A
S
E

S
T
U
D
Y*

Scenario #2:

Sherry recently found out that her employee Sam has been drinking on the job. Sherry knows that Sam has personal problems, but she can't afford to let the quality of Sam's work slip any further. Sherry is also concerned about Sam's behavior and the effect his lack of productivity will have on the other employees. To complicate things further, Sam is the nephew of the company president. Sherry wants to take the most professional approach possible. But what is it?

Assessment ...

What are the triggering events that are making it difficult for Sherry to address Sam's problem? Obviously, productivity and drinking on the job must be addressed. Sherry knows the law and the company procedures. As a professional, she would never think of allowing this to go on, but:

1. Does she really have proof, or just rumors? Is there documentation or just supposition? Often managers get angry and frustrated when they *know* something but can't do anything yet.

2. Team morale is always a concern, and it's inappropriate to discuss personnel issues publicly. Sherry may be feeling isolated and fearful about letting the team down.

3. Is Sam in a protected category? It sure is difficult to discipline the president's nephew.

Control ...

Sherry realizes that the real hot spots center on two issues: the president and team morale.

Engagement ...

Sherry decides to assemble her facts and productivity ratings on Sam and go directly to the top. By talking openly and honestly about production needs, she can see whether Sam is truly protected or whether this is just an unfounded fear. In reality, she's likely to find that the policy is clear on drinking and the need for productivity very understandable. After all, the president has as much interest in safety, production and team morale as anyone, maybe more.

Sherry also realizes she must spend more time with her people and divert some of the morale concerns. By pitching in and being part of the work team, Sherry can correct the work burden and get the true facts on Sam's performance.

Solution ...

The real problem, Sam, must ultimately be settled. Sherry has managed to play her aces in such a manner that she can now genuinely focus on what may be a very personal and long-term solution to a drinking problem.

Sherry needs to *engage* Sam face-to-face. As she looks for *solutions*, Sherry knows **denial** certainly wouldn't work here. It would make the situation worse. **Withdrawing** may be helpful to gain both perspective and information. **Placating** is inappropriate with Sam but could be used with the president, minimizing the chances of the president misinterpreting Sherry's actions.

What style should Sherry use with Sam? First, she can use the **dominance** that goes with her power as supervisor, as long as she doesn't push it too far. She definitely should not use **compromise,** because Sam needs to increase his productivity. **Collaboration** would be the best way to work toward that goal. So, in this case Sherry would begin by **withdrawing**, use **placating** with the president, and with Sam, exercise **dominance** in the short term to keep him from slipping even further; then, finally, she can use **collaboration** to work out a long-term solution.

Summary

When you use this method, you've got four ACES up your sleeve as you analyze each situation carefully and in a systematic way to determine the appropriate sequencing of your actions. You can have confidence that when you follow this objective track, you won't get derailed by the fear and anger that so easily accompany conflict. Every supervisor and manager has been dealt four aces, but too often we forget to play them.

> *Seek first to understand and only then to be understood.*

"Expect the best — and reinforce it."
Joe Batten

Here are some final tips for negotiating:

1. Remember to prepare well:
    *   Decide ahead of time what your bottom line is.
    *   Walk in the other person's shoes and imagine what he is going to say. Only then prepare your responses.
    *   Think about what the grievances are and how valid each of them is.

2. Ask yourself if you truly want to be in a cooperative relationship here. Do you want to find a middle ground on which you can both live peacefully?

3. Most importantly, go into a discussion believing that several solutions are possible, and then aim for the one that provides the most win-win solutions for all parties.

If both sides walk away from your negotiation feeling positive, progress has been made.

Questions for Personal Development

1. What is the major emphasis of this chapter?

_____

_____

_____

_____

2. What are the most important things you learned from this chapter?

_____

_____

_____

_____

3. How can you apply what you learned to your current job?

_____

_____

_____

_____

4. How will you go about making these improvements?

_____

_____

_____

_____

5. How can you monitor improvement?

_____

_____

_____

_____

6. Summarize the changes you expect to see in yourself one year from now.

_____

_____

_____

_____

3

*C*HAPTER 4

The Manager's Challenge

4

In our personal lives, in government, at work and even in recreational situations, we tend to organize ourselves into groups. In business and industry, managers have found that moving from individualized work to the team concept can bring much greater success. Organizations don't develop teams for their own sake but because teams improve and enrich performance, which ultimately improves the bottom line for a company.

Cooperation and Collaboration

Creating teams doesn't mean you'll automatically get teamwork. Teamwork happens when your people are capable of moving forward together toward a goal. It means they have the ability to turn differences and varying points of view into strengths. Is your staff cooperative? If you answer "yes," that doesn't necessarily mean you have a team. Cooperation and collaboration are very different.

Cooperation means everyone pitches in to fulfill their individual responsibilities. Collaboration means the team is committed to reaching a clear, mutually understood objective together. The success of the individual is measured by the success of the team. Team members hold each other accountable for reaching commitments.

"It takes two to speak the truth — one to speak and another to hear."
Henry David Thoreau

93

How would you describe your own staff members? Are they cooperative? Do they have the ability to collaborate?

Here are four positive characteristics that any team possesses. They will help you assess how you and your staff are doing as a team.

Power is neutral. You can handle it for good or for harm.

1. **Ownership:** If they're a team, they've established mutually agreed-upon goals. It's a misnomer to believe teams must "think up" their own goals. Goals can be drafted and proposed by anyone, but a team and all its members own the goals once they are declared. You can assess the level of ownership very quickly. Simply ask yourself, "Will everyone work, support and struggle until we've met our commitments?" Individuals have responsibilities, but when pressed, all goals in a team belong to everyone.

2. **Growth:** Team members need to learn and develop new skills on an ongoing basis in order to keep the team dynamic and flexible. Doing so means continued growth is built in. Do you see a mutual give-and-take of information among your staff members? Teams that openly share what they know with one another are able to adapt and adjust to changing priorities and shifting demands. Once a team member hoards information or becomes so specialized in her area of responsibility that no one else can act without her, problems arise. We need expertise — after all, you don't want the emergency room nurse performing the actual surgery — but there needs to be a constant updating of information and processes to demystify as much as possible the technical world we work in.

3. **Organizational success:** Individuals clearly see the bigger picture and the role their talents play in contributing to the larger organizational goals. One of the saddest commentaries on team management is to hear a team member say, "I did my job perfectly, but we still failed." The truth, is no team member is ever perfect if the team is unsuccessful!

4. **Conflict:** Team members recognize that conflict is inevitable but are able to use it to generate growth and new ideas. They also work to resolve conflict before it has a chance to fester and brew. Teamwork is typified by open, honest communication. Individuals discuss what's right and wrong with one another's work, so that goals are met. An inability to confront a team member, for fear of the repercussions, is a certain sign of team failure.

Some managers confuse having certain elements of teamwork with having a team. They think that if they have a congenial group of workers who would like to be a team and they provide occasional team-building exercises, they have a team. This may be a good start, but having these qualities doesn't necessarily constitute a team. Unless team members have a strong — almost tenacious — attitude for getting beyond their problems and disagreements, team results are poor.

Team-building exercises, programs and a cooperative environment are helpful but by themselves won't guarantee that teams will develop. They are part of the package but only one part. A team is characterized by:

- Shaping a common purpose
- Agreeing on performance goals
- Designing a common working approach
- Developing high levels of complementary skills
- Holding each member mutually accountable for results

If you intend to build a team, you must help it deal well with conflict as it occurs. If someone tells you she doesn't have conflict but is having trouble getting people to work together, you know two things for certain. First, she is having real conflict, and second, she certainly doesn't have a team.

It is impossible to put a group of dedicated people together, ask them to work at peak performance and not have conflict. Conflict is inevitable. The management challenge is to make it constructive and not just something the team endures.

> *"Three of the key elements in the art of working together are how to deal with change, how to deal with conflict and how to reach our potential."*
> Max DuPree

4

95

In fact, conflict is a very important element in the dynamics of a team. For one thing, it means you have a healthy dose of diversity in the group. But more than being an indicator, conflict is actually a team developer.

How can this be? When a team works through a conflict, it emerges as a more cohesive team. People are now connected in a different way and are sharing at a new level. Furthermore, because they've worked together on the solution, they have a high level of commitment to it. Frequently it is only after the first conflict, when the "honeymoon" of the new team ends, that the productive time together begins.

Exercise

Recall a recent conflict you faced. What did you learn from it? How did you deal with conflict? Did you learn to deal with conflict constructively?

_____

_____

_____

_____

_____

_____

_____

Conflict and Communication

What are your employees doing to each other? What are they doing for each other?

The most effective way to ensure good communication during conflict is to model what you want: openness, directness and clarity. At your team meetings, regularly ask for suggestions and air whatever resentments or problems are present. When team members see they won't be shot or hurt, they'll make confrontation of problems the norm, not the exception. Asking for both feedback and suggestions that will help ensure they're getting what they need and want while avoiding blame are critical to team success.

Managers cannot be unduly afraid of conflict or the possibility of an angry outburst. Both are likely! It's the role of the manager and every team member to move beyond the initial emotions and get to the real issues.

Believing in the process means that you have patience with your people and you trust them to solve their own problems. Believing in the process also means that, as manager, you're able to let go of control in an appropriate way and let your people make their own decisions when at all possible. It doesn't mean that you walk away from your responsibility and accountability but that you trust your team and the process you have facilitated.

A Checklist for Team Communication and Conflict Management

____ 1. Do team members openly and honestly discuss their concerns and problems?

____ 2. Is there a sense of urgency to solve problems rather than place blame?

____ 3. Do team members have a way for reporting corrections once they have been made?

____ 4. Are the specific goals toward which they're working clear and measurable?

____ 5. Is mutual accountability clear and measurable, and is there the sense that if the team fails, we all fail; if the team succeeds, we all succeed?

For each question that you answered "No," continue with the following questionnaire:

Is this a problem over which I have control? If so, what three steps can I take to correct the problem?

1. _____

2. _____

3. _____

If not, who has control and what do I need to do to influence that in this regard?

_____

_____

> *"Most breakdowns in teamwork would never happen if we remembered to treat our teammates with the basic courtesies we normally extend to customers."*
> Kenneth Kaye

4

Some frequently asked questions about team conflict

Q. What is the greatest motivator of teams?

A. Though many people believe the greatest motivator is the team leader, in fact the greatest motivator is a specific performance challenge that is clear and exciting to team members.

Q. What is the best size team?

A. Though many people believe it's any size group working together, in fact the best size is a team that's made up of 10 to 12 members. Above that number, serious problems can set in.

Q. How hard is it to develop a real team?

A. It's hard work confronting conflict while at the same time developing trust and interdependence. But these things are accomplished not by trying to become a team but more by focusing on a common challenge together.

Q. What's the most important quality for team leaders to have?

A. It may surprise you that the answer is not people skills and it's not managerial skills — it's the attitude of the team leader. The leader needs to believe strongly in the concept of the team, in the purpose of this particular team, to have trust in each person and to know when to be patient and when to take action.

Remember: The team is not an end in itself. It is the means to an end, and that end is performance. Do not allow conflict or poorly expressed anger to derail your productivity.

The Lessons of the Geese

Adapted from **Agricultural Notes**

Fact #1

When birds flock together to reach their destination, their "V" formation adds 71 percent more flying range than if each bird flew alone, because each bird creates an uplift for the ones nearby.

Lesson: People who share a common direction and a sense of belonging get where they're going faster and easier because they're uplifting each other as they go.

Fact #2

When a goose falls out of formation and suddenly feels the drag and wind resistance that comes from trying to fly alone, it will quickly get back in formation.

Lesson: If we have as much sense as a goose, we'll join others who also want to get where we're going. Conflict, anger and errors are generally self-correcting if they are allowed to be discussed openly.

Fact #3

If a lead goose becomes weary, it will drop out of the lead and let another bird take its place.

Lesson: We need to share leadership and be interdependent with others. It's a silly goose who thinks she can carry all of a team's problems alone!

Fact #4

As the geese fly they honk to encourage each other to keep up their speed.

Lesson: We need to remember to honk to each other and make sure it's encouraging. Everyone needs a good "honk" now and then, but we should hear a balance of positive and negative honks.

> *It is in the shelter of each other that people live.*
> Irish proverb

In the review below, assess your team members by circling the place on the continuum that best describes where they are.

Review: A real team has ...

1. Clear goals and expectations.
    How is my team doing on a scale of 1 to 10?
    1   2   3   4   5   6   7   8   9   10

2. A trusting relationship among the team members, so positive and negatives can be shared.
    How is my team doing on a scale of 1 to 10?
    1   2   3   4   5   6   7   8   9   10

3. Accountability to one another for reaching their goals and objectives.
    How is my team doing on a scale of 1 to 10?
    1   2   3   4   5   6   7   8   9   10

4. Skills to handle differences that surface.
    How is my team doing on a scale of 1 to 10?
    1   2   3   4   5   6   7   8   9   10

5. An attitude that includes flexibility, openness, vulnerability, responsibility and commitment.
    How is my team doing on a scale of 1 to 10?
    1   2   3   4   5   6   7   8   9   10

6. A caring attitude toward members, where support exceeds blame.
    How is my team doing on a scale of 1 to 10?
    1   2   3   4   5   6   7   8   9   10

7. Healthy and open communication. Destructive anger and bullying are rare or nonexistent.
    How is my team doing on a scale of 1 to 10?
    1   2   3   4   5   6   7   8   9   10

Analyzing and Planning
for a Team

Fill in the blanks below to focus on ways to build or improve your team.

1. What positive factors exist in my situation for creating/improving a team?

    _____

    _____

    _____

    _____

2. How can I build on them for improvement?

    _____

    _____

    _____

    _____

3. What weaknesses/obstacles are present?

    _____

    _____

    _____

    _____

4. Who/what will assist me in dealing with each of these weaknesses?

    _____

    _____

    _____

    _____

4

Combating Control and Harassment

As you have probably noticed in your own experience, problems still exist among staff members. Unfortunately, the ideal workplace doesn't exist yet. We all can work to improve relationships. Among other problems, power is often used to control others.

As you can see in the box below, there are five ways people can exert negative power against you. Some of these are very subtle tactics and not always recognized for what they are: ways to take away your control. But there are also ways you can empower yourself and others to resist and overcome controlling methods used against you. These positive actions also provide avenues for growth in yourself and those you manage.

Understanding Control

1. Demeaning labels/language	1. Choice
2. Demeaning tasks	2. Knowledge
3. Power shifts	3. Practice
4. Failure	4. Involvement
5. Self-destruction	

1. The first way people can control you is through the use of demeaning labels and language. We have all heard and perhaps even used a derogatory label to describe a person or her behavior.

   Most labels go unchallenged because they are emotion-filled. When such labels are directed at you or even to others about you, they are clear put-downs. They depersonalize and insult. Not only do they have a negative effect on you, but they are a means of controlling the listeners as well. Listeners know some other demeaning label can just as easily be used against them at any time.

Exercise

What are some negative labels you've heard to put down men, women or minorities?

Labels About Minorities Labels About Men Labels About Women

_____ _____ _____

_____ _____ _____

_____ _____ _____

_____ _____ _____

2. The second subtle tactic is the use of demeaning tasks. In reality there are no demeaning tasks per se, but there is demeaning delegation. What this means is that if you're expected to do something by virtue of your gender or are asked to do things that are generally considered beneath your rank, you're being controlled and perhaps punished. Not all tasks are created equal, and everyone knows this. When a supervisor consistently assigns the least desirable job to the same person, this is not delegating but dumping.

 At the same time, you need to be realistic. Your job primarily is to make your boss look good, and her job is to make her boss look good, and so on. However, when a person is given the not-so-subtle message that nobody else wants to do something so it's always going to be your job, even though the words are not said, the message is clear. Whether it's setting up the chairs for the meeting, dealing with a difficult client or whatever the group knows is the "dirty work," assigning it consistently to the same person is a demeaning form of control.

3. Power shifts exist when you have your power or responsibility stripped away from you solely and precisely to remind you that you are powerless. Perhaps you have been given a task, but when you succeed at it and you feel ready for more responsibility, just the opposite happens. You are not given any additional responsibility, and the new job is taken away from you. Probably one of the best examples of a power shift is when someone else steps in to take credit for your hard work and early success. This kind of control is unfair and constitutes real manipulation.

4. As hard as it may be to believe, there are people in the workplace who will set up an employee to fail. Contrary as this is to everything we as managers want to do, it is done to make a person feel dependent on the boss and drive home the point that the employee can't do anything without checking with the boss first. When you understand that the goal in the workplace is to succeed and that the more our staff succeeds, the more we succeed, the absurdity of this is clear. As you read earlier in this section, managers and supervisors should be dedicated to doing just the opposite — to affirming and giving positive feedback to set up their team members for success.

5. Another more serious problem is that of self-destruction. One kind of self-destruction is what someone does when she chooses to stop growing. This is what you do when you decide to stay inside your comfort zone and are closed off to the possibility of new growth. The person who doesn't continue to learn or read or challenge herself or attend seminars or talk with others about new ideas has chosen to stop growing. If you do this, you affect yourself and those around you, especially those working for you. This can become contagious, so that others begin to limit themselves in what they can accomplish or in the ways they can develop or learn or succeed. You know what will happen to morale, to work quality and to any team effort if this disease spreads. Whether it's your first year on the job or your last, personal growth is a hallmark of a good employee.

An extreme version of self-destructive control is someone who threatens to harm herself and uses this as a control tactic over another person. We see this in abusive relationships where the abusers threaten to harm themselves if the person being abused "abandons" them. The threat of suicide, of course, is the extreme of this kind of control tactic.

> *"Bravery is the capacity to perform properly even when scared half to death."*
> General Omar Bradley

Reexamine the previous list of five control tactics. Is there one that is a problem in your own situation? If so, describe it clearly here.

_____

_____

_____

Now, write the problem in the form of an action plan.

Action Plan

My goal(s) or objective(s):

_____

_____

_____

What steps do I need to take to accomplish this?

_____

_____

_____

Action(s) I will take:

_____

_____

_____

Now put dates next to each action step above.

How will I know when I have succeeded in this?

_____

_____

_____

What will I do to "celebrate" this success?

_____

_____

_____

4

> *"To develop a winning team, you must first of all develop a winning attitude."*
> Lou Holtz,
> Football Coach,
> Notre Dame

Positive Control Functions

Fortunately, you have internal resources available for combating the control tactics just described. You are not just a victim waiting to be pounced on by some power monger. Here are some ways to stay in charge and avoid victimization by others:

1. Your first resource is the freedom of choice. No one can control your ideas about your job. In fact, most employees have ideas about how the company could improve and what would enhance their work. As you create a climate that gives your people the freedom to express their ideas, you are unleashing the creative energy of many more people for improving your situation. This, in turn, empowers you further.

2. Knowledge is a resource that helps you expand your horizons. When you learn new things, you go outside your comfort zone. This helps you improve and gives you control over the direction of your future. Of course, you succeed when you help others grow. As you motivate and educate others, they in turn make good things happen for the whole team, and you are all more empowered and more successful. Recall a time when you learned something that improved the way you were able to do your work. Do you remember how good that felt? We all feel good when we acquire new and meaningful information, skills or insight. Growth is a wonderful experience. An important part of a supervisor's job is helping others get better through learning new things. You can do this by your own example and by providing opportunities and incentives for learning.

   Remember: A good manager works with each team member to develop her personal goals and a professional growth plan.

3. Practice is another way to put yourself in charge and even improve your life. Practice puts your ideas and knowledge into action. Practice is the means by which you *utilize*

other resources. When you practice, it means you are not just learning but using what you know. You can read through a book like this with many ideas, but the only way it can affect your world is if you practice, practice, practice, until it really becomes part of your repertoire of habits and skills. That's when it touches your life and makes something change for you.

4. Another positive source of power is staying involved in a situation. When you're disengaged from a group or situation, you can't be part of what's happening and you have no impact. When you stay involved, you become pro-active rather than passive or reactive. Your involvement stimulates the rest of your team to do the same: to take positive action. When they stay involved it creates a kind of ripple effect of positive action that affects everyone, including yourself.

The other side of involvement for you as a manager or supervisor is that, in order to foster team commitment, you need to give some of your power away, to delegate. Some people won't delegate because they fear things won't be done "right," which usually means they won't be done "their way."

Give your workers the chance to do it their way and you give them the chance to learn, to grow in confidence and maybe even show you a better way to do something. The rewards in terms of growth, morale, and team spirit are well worth it!

> *"The dogmas of the quiet past are inadequate for the stormy present and future. As our circumstances are new, we must think anew, and act anew."*
> Abraham Lincoln

4

Personal Review

As you review the four positive forces for control just discussed, put a check by the one you would most like to work on:

___ Choice

___ Knowledge

___ Practice

___ Involvement

Write for yourself three reasons why you want to develop in this way:

1. _____

2. _____

3. _____

Next, write the name of someone who can help you draw up a personal action plan for working on this:

_____

When will you meet with this person?

_____

How to Handle Harassment and Hardball Tactics

At some time you may be on the receiving end of what you perceive to be harassment or hardball tactics. Someone may consistently badger you, act in a way that is inappropriate or worse. That person has gone beyond the bounds of acceptability. It's a difficult situation in which to find yourself. When this happens, however, you can handle it effectively with the following six-step system. Notice that this system is developmental, so you need to use it in the sequence given here.

Step One: Keep yourself under control and listen

Take the time to assess what was really said and what was really meant. Often we have a knee-jerk response when someone says something that offends us or challenges our values. But an emotional response usually just brings immediate denial. Sometimes people really don't mean anything negative by what they say — that's just the way they communicate.

> *"Our fears are always more numerous than our dangers."*
> Seneca

For example, the supervisor who typically gives a "compliment" by saying something like, "That was a great job you did. What a surprise!" may not even be aware of what she's doing. Building people up and tearing them down or using sarcasm can affect them deeply. Often what we remember is not the compliment but the fact that our boss was surprised. Most of us have learned early in life that the old adage "Sticks and stones can break my bones, but words can never hurt me" is simply not true. The person who says such things may be insensitive and unaware. However, it is also possible that you're being harassed. That's why it is important for you to stop and reflect on what was said, the person who said it and what you assess was her intent.

Asking a few questions can help you accurately assess the situation. Here are some examples:

- "Let me make sure I heard you accurately …"
- "Would I be right in saying this is what you mean …"
- "I'd like to make sure we do not get off to the wrong start …"

Step Two: Make a cushion statement

Once you're clear about what was said and you've thought about the intent behind it, you can respond with a cushion statement. A cushion statement describes how you feel. Harassment is really in the eye of the beholder. What's offensive to one person may not be to another. When you make a cushion statement, you clearly and noncombatively declare your feeling about what was said.

For example: "It annoys me when you use that terminology."

An easy way to state your feelings and confront difficult situations is with the "Burger" technique (see Chapter 2). This confrontation technique is so named because your feelings (the meat) are surrounded by noncombative words (the bun). It's really three parts:

#1. Say, "When this happens ...." Attempt to avoid blame and judgmental use of the word "you." For example:

"When I hear statements like ..."

"When I'm blamed for something I know I didn't do, I ..."

"When rules are broken or people say things that intentionally hurt ..."

#2. Say, "I feel ...." It is here that you own your emotional part of the problem. Be as accurate and descriptive as you possibly can. For example:

"I feel hurt."

"I feel taken advantage of."

"I feel overwhelmed."

#3. Say, "Because ...," The last part is an explanation for why you feel the way you do. For example:

"Because I didn't deliberately harm you."

"Because I have really worked hard."

When these three parts are combined, it may sound like this: "When things are said in anger, I feel frustrated, because I'm trying hard to stay focused on the facts and not get too emotional."

You will discover that if you carry out the first two steps above, 80 percent of harassers will stop harassing.

Step Three: Explain "why"

Give the reason you feel the way you do. No one thinks or feels exactly as you do, so articulate that. What offends you may surprise the other person, who never thought of it that way. Or she may not know how she sounded, or perhaps it's just a difference in opinion about what you value. In any case, when they hear your reason for taking offense, another 10 percent of harassers will stop.

> *"People who keep a stiff upper lip find that it's damn hard to smile."*
> Judith Guest

Step Four: Look for an alternative

You don't want this incident to escalate into a major conflict, so ask the harasser some open-ended questions and put the pressure on her. Open-ended questions use one of these words: Who, how, where, what, which, why and when. They require more than a "yes" or "no" answer.

For example, you could say something like, "I'm annoyed when you use that term to describe me. It makes me feel like I'm not seen as a valued member of the team. What do you think we could do about that? How can we handle this situation more effectively so that it doesn't arise again?" When you ask a lot of open-ended questions, you throw the problem back to the other person. Remember, as soon as you get upset, you're letting her problem become your problem. That's what you want to avoid.

> *As soon as you get upset, you're letting the other person's problem become your problem.*

By now you've eliminated another 8 percent, and so only 2 percent of harassers will still be left! If the previous four sequences haven't worked, go on to the next step.

Step Five: Use the broken-record technique

The broken-record technique means that you say the same thing over and over to the other person. It's up to her to stop the broken record by giving you the acceptable answer. The acceptable answer here is "no." You say something like, "I didn't like what you said. Was it meant to hurt me?"

Will this alone make the other person stop right away? Probably not. You may have to repeat the question eight to 15 times, just like a broken record, before she finally gives you the answer you want. She'll have a number of responses, but you persist with exactly the same question until she gives you your "no." She'll probably never harass you in this way again, because manipulators don't want to be held accountable for their actions. If you confront harassers like this, chances are they'll leave you alone and find someone else to harass.

Step Six: Put it in writing

This last resort in dealing with harassment is to make a written contract — including the date, what was discussed and what was agreed upon — to get a commitment to end the harassment.

Write the facts using a format similar to the example on the next page.

First, document the date. Basically that affirms that you met. Then the other person can't "forget" that it happened. Next, summarize what was discussed and what was agreed to, so there is a clear record that can't be denied later. Finally, you both sign the document. The other person probably won't want to sign it, because she won't want to be held accountable. But it's important to have this done, so don't give up. If the other person refuses, ask her, "What would prevent you from signing this?" If you persist she'll eventually sign it, if only to get you off her back.

Remember: Behavior that is not confronted will not change. The vast majority of harassment can be stopped with the first four steps, and you may never have to use Step 6. Finally, always resolve the issue as early as possible.

If you feel you are suffering from harassment or hardball tactics, use the space on the next page to write a draft of the written contract you would like your harasser to sign. When you do this be as specific as possible. Because the final contract will include what was agreed upon with this person, this draft should contain your ideal agreement.

Be realistic and know that you are not going to fundamentally change harassers. You can only influence their behavior as it impacts you. Your most powerful information in an unpleasant situation is the knowledge that *the person who is not on the defensive is the one who is in control of the situation.* Keep yourself relaxed, on the offensive and in control by using the techniques you just learned.

Our Contract

Model

We met on_____at _____a.m./p.m.

We discussed:_____

_____

_____(current behavior).

We agreed on:_____

_____

_____(future behavior).

Signature 1._____

Signature 2._____

What About Gossip and Back-Stabbing?

Gossiping about personal matters is among the five major gaffes people make that harm their professional lives, according to business etiquette experts.

Gossip and back-stabbing are two things that disrupt work and cause unnecessary conflict and hard feelings. This kind of behavior demoralizes your staff and affects productivity. If you're being hurt by gossip and you want to stop it, there are three steps you can take to end it.

But before you do that, you have to first stop yourself from participating in gossip by refusing to listen to it, refusing to pass it on and confronting it when it happens. If you can't stop yourself from being part of the gossip problem, these steps won't work. Only when you get yourself under control do you have the right to confront it in others' gossiping.

Here are the three steps to take to end gossip.

1. When a person reports that someone is talking behind your back, ask that person to confront the gossiper with you. Say, "I can see how that would bother you. Will you go with me and talk to her together?" If her answer is "yes," you've cut off the gossip and become accountable for finding the truth. If her answer is "no," then proceed to the next step.

2. Ask if you can use the other person's name with the gossiper and repeat what she said. Then the other person is accountable for the information. Say, "It could be very uncomfortable for you to go personally, so I'll go for you, but I must have permission to use your name. OK?" If her answer is "no," proceed to the next step.

3. Say clearly and directly to this person, "Then this isn't true, and I'll do all I can to ignore and discredit this rumor." After that, most people will hesitate to come to you with gossip. This takes you out of the gossip loop or sequence in the future.

However, if you are a supervisor and someone comes to you with information about an employee, you may have to take action. If it has nothing to do with work, you can simply respond, "I don't care to hear about this." If it is affecting her work, you need to confront the employee. Tell her what you've heard and listen to her response. Do not involve the person who came to you with the information. If there's a problem with your employee, ask some open-ended questions such as, "How can we handle this?" Determine the best way to handle the problem and end the gossip as soon as possible.

Will these procedures stop all the gossip and back-stabbing? Of course not, but you'll give gossipers one fewer person to talk to and you'll stop the flow when it hits you. As a manager or supervisor you are also signaling what kind of behavior you condone.

4

Exercise

In the space below, write the personal resolution you want to make about gossip. It may be to stop listening or participating. It may be to confront a particular person the next time she comes to you or it may be to take action with an employee about whom you've been told some work-related information. Whatever you decide, be very specific in what you want to do and when you want to do it.

_____

_____

_____

_____

_____

_____

_____

_____

_____

Taking "Time-Out" for Anger

The ancient philosopher Aristotle talked about anger as the energy that enables us to face difficulty. As uncomfortable as many of us are with anger, it is a necessary part of our lives. As we discussed in Chapter 1, being angry comes from how we interpret some kind of physiological arousal.   Whether we experience butterflies in our stomach, become tense and rigid or experience other physical symptoms, we give an interpretation or meaning to what has occurred. Here is an illustration:

Scenario #1:

Imagine that you're in a department store at the mall during the Christmas Eve rush. Once again you've waited until the eleventh hour to shop, and there are mobs of people everywhere. After work you pull into the crowded parking lot. You've cruised around for 20 minutes, just missing three parking spaces because someone zipped in ahead of you. Finally, you locate a space at the far end of the lot. You make your way through the mall to the department store and locate the department you need. But you can't find the right size in the gift you're buying. There are no sales clerks available. You settle on another item, but the only available color is one your friend wouldn't be caught dead in. A sense of frustration and anger is building up. Finally, you select an entirely different gift and, with a sense of disappointment, take your place in the long checkout line. People are hot, tired and impatient ... crying children and poking elbows seem to be everywhere. Someone steps on your foot and another person jostles you with her package. Now you are aware that you are really angry.

Scenario #2:

Later that evening you've joined your teenagers and the local high school parents' club at the stadium for a Holiday Extravaganza Celebration. You're still tired, and you didn't have time for supper because of your shopping. The traffic into the parking lot is bumper-to-bumper, and people are honking and waving

> *"A little righteous anger really brings out the best in the American personality. Our nation was born when 56 patriots got mad enough to sign the Declaration of Independence."*
> Lee Iacocca

4

to each other. Band members with tubas are squeezing between the traffic trying to get into the stadium. The loudspeakers are blaring holiday music, and friends are shouting to each other to come sit together. You begin to feel your heart pumping as you get caught up in the noisy atmosphere. As the line snakes through the turnstile, people jostle and bump each other. Someone steps on your now sore foot, but you laugh it off.

Physically these experiences are similar and they are both capable of eliciting the same kinds of feelings. But as pointed out in an earlier chapter, feelings come from thoughts. We think our own thoughts; therefore, we choose our feelings. In the two cases described here, you interpret similar experiences in entirely different ways. The first one makes you angry, the second uplifts your spirits.

One technique that is helpful in our personal and professional lives is to take "time-out" before anger bubbles to the point where we might lose control. Time-out is a technique that many parents use when their children are fighting with each other or misbehaving in a group. It works for adults, too. Time-out simply means that you remove yourself from a situation that is irritating you momentarily, in order to interrupt your anger. The technique provides breathing room, so you can come back later and deal with the problem in a healthy way.

> *"We have met the enemy, and he is us."*
> Pogo

Intense anger can lead to verbal and physical abuse. Removing yourself both physically and mentally (don't let your mind work over the problem while you're taking a time-out) allows you to keep an irritation from escalating into uncontrolled behavior. Returning later to deal with what made you angry is important, as long as you're able to do it in a calm manner. If you're not, repeat the same time-out process again.

Violence

As someone who deals with other people in your work, you need to appreciate how quickly anger and frustration can escalate into rage and even explode into violence. Many people today are coping with many simultaneous factors that contribute to the rise of violence. Never before have they had to deal with so much change happening at such a fast pace. People don't have a chance to manage transitions, which contributes to their feeling of life being out of control.

Other factors include increased responsibility at home and increased pressure for productivity in the workplace. The cumulative stress from day-to-day living, combined with chronic fear, causes some people to live in a heightened state of physical arousal that can easily erupt into a violent response. Often the immediate cause of such an eruption is seemingly trivial but is the proverbial straw that broke the camel's back. People are most likely to react with violence when they feel they have no control or when they have no effective way of expressing their anger. As a workplace manager, you cannot solve social problems, but you can help your employees learn to deal with anger and conflict appropriately within the work context. You can teach the techniques in this book and make sure they are used in your workplace. When you do this you are being a good manager and also a good leader. These skills will serve your workers both on the job and in society.

"Hating people is like burning down your own home to get rid of the rat."
Harry Emerson

Questions for Personal Development

1. What is the major emphasis of this chapter?

_____

_____

_____

_____

2. What are the most important things you learned from this chapter?

_____

_____

_____

_____

3. How can you apply what you learned to your current job?

_____

_____

_____

_____

4. How will you go about making these improvements?

_____

_____

_____

_____

5. How can you monitor improvement?

_____

_____

_____

_____

6. Summarize the changes you expect to see in yourself one year from now.

_____

_____

_____

_____

119

4

CHAPTER 5

Self-Care Spells Success

Managing Conflict and Anger Is a Process

5

Some people think of their lives as a journey rather than a series of snapshots. Their lives are a series of paths they've traveled and continue to travel year by year, day by day. This outlook sees life's experiences as part of a continuum.

You can view handling conflict as an ongoing journey, a road you're on, rather than as specific events to be dealt with. This approach is valuable in two ways. First, as we pointed out at the very beginning of this book, conflict is part of daily human experience. It is not something that happens and then disappears. It will always be with you in varying degrees and in all the various aspects of your life. Get used to the idea of living with conflict. Don't try to deny it or run away from it. It's here to stay. Some people try to ignore it or resent having to face conflict and look for someone to blame for it. Others feel it's unfair. However, if you accept conflict as a "given," you can put your energy into learning to deal with it rather than waste your energy resenting it or trying to escape from it.

> *There can be no progress in the workplace until an individual values himself and feels valued by others.*

Conflict is also a process in the sense that, just as conflicts change, so does your capacity to deal with them in a skillful way. You have learned new insights and skills, and as you practice them in the real world, your ability to handle conflict will improve. You are engaged in a process, on a journey. This journey has a starting point and a destination:

Starting point ▥➡ ▥➡ ▥➡ ▥➡ ▥➡ ▥➡ ▥➡ ▥➡ **Destination**

You decide how far you want to go in developing your conflict management skills. You already have a lot of knowledge to act on. You know you can learn and you can improve, but it's up to you.

Likewise, you have certain wants such as love, control and self-esteem, which you learned in the earlier chapters form the basis of your feelings of satisfaction. As your wants are met, of course, your satisfaction increases.

Wants ▥➡ ▥➡ ▥➡ ▥➡ ▥➡ ▥➡ ▥➡ ▥➡ **Satisfaction**

In order to be aware of your growth in getting your needs met, you need to look back and remind yourself of the progress you have made. When you stop to acknowledge how far you've come, you feel a sense of satisfaction, happiness and well-being. That's important in two ways. First, it helps you feel happy about your life and recognize your growth. Secondly, it provides you with the encouragement and the motivation to continue down the path of growth you've embarked upon.

Goal-Setting

Part of this process includes setting goals and achieving them.

Goals ▥➡ ▥➡ ▥➡ ▥➡ ▥➡ ▥➡ ▥➡ ▥➡ **Achievement**

Goal-setting is one of the most important steps you must take on the road to growth and development. If you want to accomplish something, you have to define it for yourself. If you don't define your goal, you won't even know when you've reached it.

"Life's a continuous business, and so is success, and it requires continuous effort."
Margaret Thatcher

5

122

If learning to deal with conflict is important to you, setting goals for yourself will go a long way toward getting you there. Sometimes our goals are so big and so general that they scare us and seem impossible to attain. That's why it's important not only to set large goals or long-term goals but to break them down into smaller goals, or objectives. This way you can work through your process one step at a time and not be defeated by the enormity of the goal. When you reach one of your objectives along the way, it also helps give you a feeling of accomplishment. Stop to acknowledge and reward yourself at these intervals, and it will help you move forward in the process.

Handling conflict is also part of the process toward resolution.

Conflict ⅢⅢ➡ ⅢⅢ➡ ⅢⅢ➡ ⅢⅢ➡ ⅢⅢ➡ ⅢⅢ➡ ⅢⅢ➡ ⅢⅢ➡ **Resolution**

While we know that conflict can lead to resolution, we also know conflict doesn't always do so. But by setting goals and by using the knowledge in this manual, you are moving ahead, making progress in that direction, and you are doing all you can to contribute to positive resolution.

5

The Proactive Manager

Have you ever felt like you're a little paper boat on a stormy sea? That's the kind of feeling you get when your life is out of control. One of the reasons this happens is that you're reacting to outside forces that are buffeting and pushing you this way and that, deciding where *they* want you to go. You probably know people whose lives are like this — adrift without goals or destinations.

> *Conflict can indeed direct a company, a department or a manager.*

Imagine if your company was like that: no goals or sense of direction, so that it simply reacted to whatever came along. You wouldn't think much of the management of such a company. But, somehow, when it comes to conflict, people expect to "fly by the seat of their pants" with no plan and no direction to the process, simply reacting to whatever others decide to do. If you let it, conflict can indeed direct a company, a department or a manager.

Clear Decisions

During conflict your people look for decisive action. They look to you to decide what to do and where to go. When you have specific goals, you appear decisive, and that makes them feel secure and confident in your leadership.

Managers need goals and directions not only for their departments but also for dealing with conflict. In conflict you need to know where you're going!

Here are some important questions to think about.

1. Am I sure of myself?
2. Have I understood the company and its policies well enough to respond as a manager?
3. If I am wrong is there room to learn from my errors?
4. Are my actions consistent with my management philosophy?
5. Am I willing to allow outsiders to help me in the conflict? (This question is an excellent test, because if you're worried about looking good, you may have escalated the conflict!)

Tolerance for Diversity

"A great many people think they are thinking when they are merely rearranging their prejudices."
William James

Diversity among staff members is often the source of conflict. People have different ideas, perspectives and ways of doing things. All of these can cause conflict. Yet, diversity is a rich natural resource for any organization. How boring and static it would be if we all thought the same! So, how do we deal with this tension? Problems arise from diversity when alternatives are seen as a threat. The atmosphere and the degree of tolerance toward diversity will vary with the issues and people involved.

When you as a manager or supervisor can appreciate diversity, you are free to manage the environment, not the diversity. You encourage hearing different ideas and view them as a resource. While your employees want their leaders to be decisive, they don't want them to be dictatorial. The way around this dilemma is to balance your decisiveness with a tolerance for diversity. When you allow competing ideas in your workplace without being threatened by them, you become a powerful leader. When you are clear about your management philosophy and where you are going, it is easier to let go of the defensiveness that is intolerant of different philosophies.

Conflict Management Reduces Aggression

Confidence comes from knowing and accepting your strengths and your limitations — not depending on affirmation from others.

As you manage the environment of your workplace, you need to watch for certain reactions in yourself. One of the defense mechanisms that can be triggered during conflict is aggression. When you behave aggressively toward someone, he is very likely to respond aggressively. Now you have two or more equally aggressive responses, which, of course, rapidly escalates the conflict. A manager who behaves in this way is often perceived as unfair, capricious or as making decisions with no real cause or foundation.

When you sense you're being aggressive, examine the underlying issues:
- Is this a common reaction for me in these situations?
- Do I have a point to prove or an ax to grind?
- Is this energy properly directed for the event?
- Do other people have this same reaction?

Closely related to aggression is anger. Remember, as you read previously, anger is a secondary emotion. If someone criticizes the quality of your work, you may respond angrily, but your primary emotion was that you felt belittled and that your abilities were questioned.

Sometimes anger and aggression are useful and important at work. For example, if you must deal with a difficult person and the event requires firm, clear intentions, aggression can be an ally. But remember: You must choose the aggressive style deliberately and consciously, not find yourself caught up in a reactive emotion.

5

How you communicate your message is important. The following words signal aggressiveness and may prompt a negative reaction. Use these words when you choose to give an aggressive response, and delete them when you're dealing with potential conflict.

- You must (ought, should, had better)
- You always/you never
- Don't ask why, just do it
- You know better than that

Exercise

Think of a time when it would be appropriate to use one of the above phrases with your employees.

_____

_____

What is an example of inappropriate use of these phrases?

_____

_____

_____

During conflict, you can soften aggressive messages by using the following techniques:

1. **Remember to share the responsibility.** It's hard to be combative with someone who's on your side.

2. **Encourage listening; be informed.** It's amazing how much you can discover if you pay attention to what others are saying.

3. **Watch for excessive self-interest.** Winning is for everyone. A title or position may give you control over people, but true authority involves respect. Respect must be earned. Dictatorial leadership is not conducive to a team philosophy.

4. **Realize that anger is short-lived for most aggressive people.** There are individuals, however, who don't forget. Enemies created during the resolution of one conflict may be around for the next.

Conflict Management Reduces Passive Behavior

Often those who should be leading are passive and weak. One characteristic of passive management is the tendency to gloss over things, which results in the loss of respect of co-workers. If you have a passive style, you're more effective during lower stages of conflict, because the coping strategies of avoidance and obliging tend to be passive in nature. However, during higher levels of conflict, those same actions will simply make you look feeble.

The passive style of conflict management often gives the appearance of being removed and unaffected by what's happening. In fact, though, the passive manager is usually frustrated during intense conflict. This outward appearance can be calming, but it is very important that the passive manager communicate that he is indeed coping with the problem and that the issues are being dealt with. At times you must be direct and deliberate and simply say, "It may look like I'm not doing much now, but I care and am going to find the best options for everyone."

The passive manager may feel out of control when he experiences fear, anxiety and guilt. One technique for enhancing self-control if this happens is to remind yourself how conflict fits into the big picture — the overall direction your department is moving in.

> *"Of all the traps and pitfalls in life, self-disesteem is the deadliest ... summed up in the phrase, 'It's no use, I can't do it.' "*
> Maltx

5

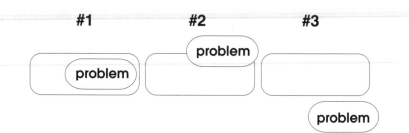

Decide whether this problem is part of the big picture as in #1. Perhaps the conflict is only one aspect of the big picture, as in drawing #2. Other times you'll determine that the conflict is not related to the big picture, as in diagram #3. This will help you keep it in perspective, which, in turn, enables you to feel and act in control.

A passive manager is likely to use the following statements, which may cause a counterproductive reaction:

- I wish ...
- If only ...
- I'm sorry, but ...
- This is probably wrong ...

Here are some ideas to help enhance your style if you are a passive manager:

1. **Use direct communication (face-to-face) when possible.** This demonstrates that you are involved. Learn to face people whether you are saying difficult things or not, but especially if you are giving bad news. Even if you need to present a written record or memo, you can still talk to the person about its content.

   It will be helpful to remember that the most seasoned conflict management specialist feels uncomfortable at times like this. You can be confident that you are feeling the same things the other party is feeling.

"The meek ain't gonna inherit nothin' west of Chicago."
from *The Quick and the Dead*

Shyness, lack of confidence or feeling intimidated can be overcome through practice and by assuming the opposite characteristics. If you appear withdrawn, you leave yourself open to misinterpretation. Resentment can build easily when you don't communicate directly, and lack of respect for your leadership will be hard to overcome once your employees decide you lack confidence.

> *Eagerness to agree can be interpreted in the same way as appearing withdrawn.*

2. **Take time.** Don't respond immediately with agreement. Eagerness to agree can be interpreted in the same way as appearing withdrawn. People may assume you are intimidated or you have lost confidence. Quick agreement is also interpreted as not caring enough to think things through. Even though you may still come to the same conclusion after thinking things over, give yourself time or risk being misjudged. In fact, sometimes you may come to another conclusion after thinking things over again away from the pressure of the moment. Use conditional agreement as a bridge between your point and theirs. For example: "You've made some valid points; I'd like to put them in proper perspective."

3. **Practice active listening.** Interrupt and ask clarifying or probing questions. Be part of the event. Some people are natural introverts or listeners and can appear to be disengaged when they're really taking things in carefully. Ask questions, even if you think you know the answer. This helps you test your assumptions and makes you part of what's going on. Did you ever see someone in a group discussion who keeps his eyes down and doodles? What might people be assuming about him? While it may not be a fair assumption on their part, part of your job is to give the clear message to your employees that you are interested and engaged. Whether you are listening or speaking, be sure to maintain good direct eye contact with the speaker.

5

4. **Watch for guilt.** Guilt is an early warning sign that insecurities exist and that the conflict requires a more active management style. When you feel responsible or feel like you're to blame, see this as a signal that you might be feeling insecure and that you need to take action. Analyze the situation and use the methods you learned in this book. To become more secure and assertive, it helps to seek advice from others who are more experienced.

5. **Listen to yourself.** Speak in a voice that is confident and that doesn't rise at the end of a statement as though it were a question.

Voice coaches tell us that people project an impression of authority or insecurity with the first few sentences they speak. Often women in particular sound tentative and as though they're asking a question whenever they speak. Studies show this greatly affects how seriously their ideas are taken. Role-play a situation you are facing, and tape-record yourself. Then play the tape back, and see if this sounds like someone who is a confident manager.

People under stress generally raise the pitch and tone of their voice. By controlling the sound of your voice, you can at least give the appearance of confidence and control under pressure. Lower your voice and slow down to gain control of yourself.

"What is the use of running if we're not on the right road?"
German proverb

5

Self-Assessment

How would you rate yourself as a manager?

Circle the appropriate response.

1. Face-to-Face Communication

   Need Improvement: not at all — somewhat — definitely

   | 1 | 2 | 3 | 4 | 5 |

2. Taking Time

   Need Improvement: not at all — somewhat — definitely

   | 1 | 2 | 3 | 4 | 5 |

3. Active Listening

   Need Improvement: not at all — somewhat — definitely

   | 1 | 2 | 3 | 4 | 5 |

4. Feeling Guilty

   Need Improvement: not at all — somewhat — definitely

   | 1 | 2 | 3 | 4 | 5 |

5. Speaking Confidently

   Need Improvement: not at all — somewhat — definitely

   | 1 | 2 | 3 | 4 | 5 |

5

Recovering Self-Esteem

You should be able to see that all of the systems for dealing with conflict and anger will fail if you don't take care of yourself. You are responsible for maintaining your self-esteem along the path of conflict management.

Nothing hurts more than words harshly spoken, especially by someone we respect or consider to be a friend. Recovering your self-respect is important after conflict. The good news about self-esteem is that we can get it back when it's been lost or damaged. And it's crucial for you to recover your confidence or self-esteem once anger has been vented. How? You need to pay attention to these five specific areas of your life.

1. *Behavior.* You have needs that are very important. As discussed earlier, these include: the need to be loved, the need for control and the need for self-esteem. Get in touch with your dominant need. For most people it's control. If your needs are not being met, rather than try to change your needs, change what you are doing to get them. Change your actions and do something you know gives you a sense of control. Spend time with someone you love, or do something you do well. The path to self-esteem is clearest when you follow what has worked and do what you like, rather than try to fix something that's broken or uncomfortable.

Exercise

Ask yourself:

What's my most dominant need?

_____

_____

_____

What actions will help me meet that need?

_____

_____

_____

2. *Feelings.* Get used to describing your feelings rather than expressing them. This allows you to tell people what you feel and what you need.

Get in touch with specific emotions you're feeling, and accept those emotions rather than deny them. Respecting your feelings is a vital aspect of self-esteem. Don't "beat yourself up" for emotions you experience. You should be your greatest coach and cheerleader, not your greatest critic. A helpful first step for someone who is not attuned to his feelings is to stop several times a day and simply ask: "What am I feeling?"

If you hear yourself saying, "I'm afraid" or "I'm angry," remember that these are usually secondary emotions. Probe deeper and discover the emotions and feelings that lie underneath the fear or anger.

3. *Develop "PMA," a positive mental attitude.* Some people carry around an "NMA," or negative mental attitude. A person with an NMA wallows in his misery and blames everyone else for it. This is the person who responds to, "Good morning!" with "What's good about it?" He answers the question, "How are you doing?" with "What do you care?" He answers your "See you next week," with "Thanks for the warning." He is so busy having a miserable life that he can't feel good about himself. It takes work and a conscious effort to be positive in the midst of a negative environment. A negative attitude is the enemy if you care about your self-esteem. Every day, examine your mental outlook or attitude. Put a note on your bathroom mirror or daily calendar that asks: "How's my PMA today?"

4. *Beliefs.* Your beliefs provide direction. Your first beliefs are about humanity in general: You either believe that people are basically good or basically evil. That impacts how you relate to others, if you trust others and how you get along with others. Get in touch with your basic beliefs about people. Do you assume that each person is good? Do you assume that people are basically out for themselves and in competition with you?

> *"Our deeds determine us, as much as we determine our deeds."*
> George Eliot

5

> *Good plans shape good decisions.*

Exercise

Ask yourself:

What do I believe about humanity and how does that affect my dealings with others?

_____

_____

_____

Your second set of beliefs is about a higher order or an absence of one. This determines your values and how you conduct your life. Think about the basic or fundamental principles that drive your life. What is it that, underneath it all, determines what you do with your life?

Your third set of beliefs has to do with life itself and whether you view it as fair or unfair. There are some people who believe that life is basically giving them a raw deal and giving others a good deal. Such people see themselves as victims. They go around complaining about what he's got or what she's got or what they've got. If you asked them if life is supposed to be fair, they'd shout, "Yes! Of course! And it's not fair to me." They are sour on life and act as though they're waiting for a better life to come along. How much better to have an attitude that says, "If I've only got one mortal life, I've got to make it the best one I possibly can!" and then go about putting effort into making this the best possible life. You can make the most of this life by making the most of this day.

Exercise

Do I tend to compare my life with others and feel I was not dealt as good a hand? How does this overflow into my attitudes and how good I feel about myself?

_____

_____

_____

Your fourth set of beliefs has to do with your belief in yourself. This means you believe in yourself as someone you like or someone you basically dislike. This belief affects not only how you treat yourself but how you treat others. If you have a conviction that you are good and capable, that will be a self-fulfilling prophecy. It gives you tremendous power. Have you ever been around someone who was constantly bad-mouthing himself? Maybe he doesn't like what he does, who he is, where he lives, to whom he's married — and he'll tell you about it all the time. That's a good example of how a person's self-image impacts himself and those around him. People don't want to be around such a person because his attitude is not only unpleasant and depressing but can be contagious.

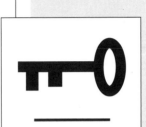

Remember, when you aren't experiencing success or you aren't feeling good about yourself, check (and adjust, if necessary) your four belief systems.

5. *Programming your self-talk.* To reclaim and build your self-esteem, every day put a positive diskette in the computer of your brain. Type on your diskette, "This is going to be a good day." Have you ever missed a good day because you had a negative attitude? Positive programming builds positive beliefs. These positive beliefs develop into attitudes that then create positive feelings, which produce positive behaviors. See how it all fits together? See how much control over yourself you really have? But every day, others may try to put different diskettes in your disk drive, diskettes that are negative and the opposite of what you want and need. You want to develop a permanent lock on your disk-drive door for negative diskettes.

In other words, you can be about as happy as you choose to be. You can affect how you feel about yourself and others. You can affect your behavior and build the kind of life you want, one day at a time. When you feel happy and content, you can take credit. If you're miserable and discontented, you can't blame anyone else. Do you know someone who seems happy with himself and happy with his life? Ask him to tell you his secret.

Remember: No system for handling conflict and managing anger can work if you haven't first learned how to take care of yourself and to maintain your self-esteem along the path to success.

Personal Power Through Self-Talk

You may not be aware of it, but as you go through each day you are engaged in a continuous conversation. That conversation is with yourself. What you say to yourself has a great influence on your attitudes and behavior. Every day you program your brain with one of four levels of self-talk:

1. "I can't"
2. "I should"
3. "I will no longer" and, most importantly,
4. "I choose to"

Most people spend 80 percent of their self-talk telling themselves what they can't do or saying negative things to themselves. They spend only about 20 percent giving themselves positive messages. It's your option to choose which it will be for you.

Level One Self-Talk: "I can't"

In the first level of self-talk, you say to yourself or about yourself, "I can't." When was the last time you said that? What was it about? People tell themselves every day that they can't lose weight, they can't pass the test, they can't complete the assignment on time, they can't break a habit, even that they can't stop saying they can't.

Level Two Self-Talk: "I should"

The next level of negative self-talk is the famous "I should." Some people go around every day "shoulding" on themselves ... "I should lose weight, I should get up earlier, I should read that book, I should learn to deal with conflict better." What were some "shoulds" you have said to yourself recently? Level Two self-talk tends to be trapped in the past, and although you can rarely alter the past or its results, the " I shoulds" keep you powerless.

5

Level Three Self-Talk: "I will no longer"

When you move to the next level, you are making the giant leap into the 20 percent of positive messages. This third level of self-talk is the "I will no longer." Here you begin telling yourself that you'll stop a particular habit, behavior, way of thinking, etc. You might say, "I will no longer start the day with a negative attitude; I will stop leaving late for work; I will stop eating dessert for the next week ..." See how this is a step up? It is a conscious decision to stop something undesirable rather than telling yourself that you "can't" or you "should" do it. You're making a positive decision to cut out part of your undesirable behavior.

Level Four Self-Talk: "I choose to"

The most influential form of self-talk is Level Four, "I choose to." At this level you consciously move in a positive new direction. You're taking charge of your life. It is at this level that you set powerful, positive goals. It's here that you are stating that you choose to change. Some people make positive, affirmative statements to themselves such as, "I am capable of change" or "I am responsible for this."

It's important to reach Level Four and correct negative images about yourself, or nothing positive will happen as a result of your self-talk. Sometimes the fear of the unknown makes us less than enthusiastic about change because it feels scary. Not knowing what the change will bring can tempt you to stay with what you know, even if it's not what you want.

"I will take an action." Say this to yourself every day, adding the action you have chosen. So, how do you know where to begin with your positive self-talk? Begin by setting one goal you want to accomplish. Think about your self-esteem and your self-talk. What can you do at this time to improve them? Take a look at where you are not; self-assess and set goals for yourself. It's amazing how many people never set goals. Goals are a positive indicator of a self-directed person, a leader. In setting your goals, it's important to follow the process outlined on the next page.

> *"I am not going to limit myself just because people won't accept the fact that I can do something else."*
> Dolly Parton

5

Personal Goal-Setting

1. **State your goal in the present tense.** State your goal as if you already have accomplished it. Describe what it looks like when you've already accomplished it. For example, "I get up 20 minutes early each day so I'm not stressed by the traffic." Or, "I set aside time at 4 o'clock on Friday to review and plan the week."

2. **Be very specific about your goal, and put it in writing.** These techniques work together to make it possible for you to succeed. A vague, general goal is one that will not get accomplished. A goal written down is a goal that has new power.

3. **Make a simple, easy-to-use plan.** The more complicated it is, the less likely you are to use it. It's easy to abandon or find reasons not to work on something that's complicated or that feels overwhelming. Even though you don't always succeed under the best of circumstances, with a clear, simple plan you'll always be on track.

4. **Be practical about what you can achieve.** Don't set yourself up to fail by expecting too much. Remember to reward yourself along the way, so you mark the steps of accomplishment.

5. **Be very personal and honest.** Ask yourself, "Do I need the help of others in accomplishing this goal? How am I going to get the help I need?"

6. **Make sure the goal demands enough of you and is challenging.** None of us ever reaches our full potential. We need to challenge ourselves if we don't want to stay where we are. How big do you want to grow in this lifetime? Don't sell yourself short and settle for a less full and rich life than you need to.

Exercise

Begin reprogramming your brain with positive self-talk. In the space below, write three "I choose to" statements that will begin to program a new and positive direction for your life.

1) I choose to _____

_____

2) I choose to _____

_____

3) I choose to _____

_____

5

Rejection and Toxic Stressors

When you're feeling overwhelmed or rejected, or if you have excessive stress in your life, it will manifest itself in a number of ways. It's important to pay attention when this happens and deal with what's going on. Sometimes, in the midst of difficulties, you can be so caught up in solving the causes of stress that you don't realize the toll it is taking on you. Here are some warning signals to watch for that signal when you are becoming a victim of excessive stress.

1. Fear of Failure

The first sign that stress may be overtaking you is that you feel you have no alternatives and you begin to fear failure. When you are afraid of failing, you become tempted to do nothing. To achieve success means you have to take risks. You may feel that regardless of what you do, you're going to fail. What happens? Your sense of helplessness produces inaction, which guarantees failure. It's a vicious circle. You may also overanalyze to the point of paralysis, which is a form of avoidance; you put your energy into thinking instead of acting.

139

Having decided there is no viable course of action, you feel you're in a lose-lose situation, so you say and do nothing.

2. Complaining

Another trap to avoid is complaining. It's common for anyone to complain occasionally, but when your complaints escalate and your perspective turns critical, you have fallen into a toxic situation. Complaining is truly an exercise in futility, because half the people you work with don't care about your problem, and the others are just glad you have the problem instead of them. More importantly, complaining is self-destructive because your mind is continually occupied with negative thoughts. Find out why you're complaining so much by looking at the circumstances of your life.

Often what we're complaining about is not really what's bothering us. If you have a chronic feeling of dissatisfaction and constantly complain, take a hard look at what's really going on. That way you break the complaining habit and clear your mind for more positive and productive thoughts.

3. Wishing

Grasping at straws is when you find yourself wishing or hoping that your conflict or problem will go away. "I wish he would change," "I hope they stop fighting," etc. Does conflict ever go away on its own? Rarely, so chances are against it happening now. Wishing and hoping is a last-ditch attempt. Instead, you need to take action. Restart your wishes as specific goals and positive self-talk. The real problem with wishing is that it often substitutes for real actions. The person caught wishing often believes he's doing more than he really is.

4. Self-Defeating Behavior

Do you find yourself abandoning projects soon after you begin? Are you afraid of completing the task? Often people fall into this trap because they are afraid of being judged harshly on their final product. Perfectionists, on the other hand, will start a project but have difficulty concluding it, because they are continually improving, trying to make the final product perfect. Both of these are self-defeating behaviors guaranteed to destroy self-confidence. If you never complete a project, you *never* experience success. If you never experience success, you never

> *"I have found that if I have faith in myself and in the idea I am tinkering with, I usually win out."*
> Charles K. Kettering

5

achieve self-esteem and eventually you self-destruct. On the other hand, when you finish a job you have a real sense of accomplishment and you reinforce your ability to succeed. This builds confidence instead of tearing it down.

5. Back at Square One

Have you ever been in the midst of a project and discovered that the specifications you were given were incorrect? Has one of your staff members dropped the ball on his part of the project that was then overdue? These incidents are similar to the feeling you get when you lose an important document on your computer after working on it all day. This is what it's like to be at square one again and wonder if you have the strength to start over. When that happens, it's normal to feel frustrated and upset. But if you wake up in the morning feeling totally helpless and defeated, think about it again. We all have good days and bad days. In a very real sense, every one of us starts at square one every single morning. Every day is a new day. One successful NFL coach tells his players that win or lose, the game is over at midnight. Put it away and start tomorrow fresh. Like Scarlett O'Hara said in the midst of her trials, "Tomorrow is another day." When you've had a bad day, you need to give yourself the gift of a new attitude as part of receiving the gift of a new day. The ability to re-create yourself daily is essential to avoid frustration, burnout and negative feelings.

"When a thing is done, it's done. Don't look back. Look forward to your next objective." General George C. Marshall

6. Unwilling to Change

Sometimes being unwilling or afraid to change disguises itself as self-pity. Have you ever heard people using the excuse that they can't do something because they're too old to change? Do you know someone who excuses himself from trying something by saying, "You just don't understand." There are so many examples of people, including the elderly, doing new things, learning and growing, that it's absurd to try to hide behind the false excuse of age. When you find yourself fighting new systems and new ideas, see it as a red flag warning you of a problem you need to look into. You can't change the past; you can change the future, but to change your future, you have to take some action today.

When you display any of these behaviors, you need to realize you're resisting your own feelings and conscience. Stress causes you to react instead of act. That's when you lose control. You want to have a peaceful inner world in order to handle conflicts in the outer world.

Anger and Expectations

> *"Life's under no obligation to give us what we expect."*
> Margaret Mitchell

One of the most powerful internal forces that influences your behavior is your expectations. Did you ever have someone carry out an assignment so well that you were surprised and elated? Now think of a time when someone's performance truly disappointed you, perhaps so much that you felt really angry at him. In each case you had certain expectations about his behavior or his work. In both cases the outcomes that you anticipated reflected your own standards, and those standards "set you up" for disappointment or for happiness. What this says is that expectations can make you more prone to feeling angry both at yourself and at others.

High expectations can lead to anger. People who are perfectionists or are critical will commonly experience more frustration and anger because they are continually being disappointed. Their employees can rarely achieve their high expectations. They feel as though people are always letting them down. But the performance that disappoints them most often is their own.

It's easy to see how having high expectations causes disappointment, but, ironically, it is also true that low expectations can lead to anger. Why? Because lack of self-confidence heightens your frustration level and makes you more likely to react angrily to a situation. If you think you can't handle a job or a situation, if you're predicting failure for yourself, your frustration level is raised, and you increase your chances of becoming angry. So, what's a person to do? Clearly, the problem is having unrealistic expectations: too high or too low — so the solution lies in working to establish realistic expectations of yourself and of others.

Realistic Expectations

As discussed earlier, two signals of unrealistic expectations are the word "should" and the words "never" or "can't." When you hear yourself "shoulding," e.g., "I should have; you should have," that signals that expectations may have been too high. On the other side, when you say, "We can't; I'll never be able to," it may signal that you're underestimating your abilities and expecting too little.

Here are three tips to help you determine whether you have realistic expectations:

1. *Compare your current expectations or goals to your past record or experience.* Have you done anything similar to this in the past? What does that experience tell you about what to expect now? Some examples: On what basis can you expect sales to increase 35 percent this year, when the best year ever was 17 percent? Your department is doubling for the second time in four years. How many new customer service clerks did you hire last time, and what does that tell you about new hires now? You are giving your staffers a new project. How long did it take them to complete a similar assignment last month?

2. *Use others to test your expectations.* Talk with others. Get advice from people you respect about whether they think your expectations are too high or too low. Use their experience for comparison. An open and honest exploration of your hopes, dreams, plans and demands on others will help you objectively review your expectations.

3. *Test whether you really believe you're being realistic.* Make a percentage "bet" with yourself on the outcome. What chance do you really think you have of succeeding in this? Perhaps 20 percent, 50 percent, 80 percent? That gives you a kind of "gut level" barometer about whether your expectations are too high or too low.

    It's easy to set yourself up for "justifiable anger" when you predict outcomes beyond realistic attainment. Some people project success for themselves that is too remote to attain. Others set up their teammates, peers or spouse for failure by excessive demands. In either case, learn to recognize the predictable outcomes you create.

> *"When nothing is sure, everything is possible."*
> Margaret Drabble

5

Be Clear About Expectations

Whenever there is more than one person involved in accomplishing something, clarity is always a critical success factor. Do you assume the other person understands your expectations? Are you assuming that he agrees with these expectations? If so, you are surely setting yourself up for trouble. Clarity and communication are essential for good relationships, productivity and keeping unnecessary anger to a minimum. Spell out your expectations, and confirm that others share this understanding.

Determining whether your expectations are realistic can be a great help in taking care of yourself. Use the advice above if you find yourself frequently disappointed or chronically angry or unsure about whether you're expecting too much or too little of yourself and your staff.

Clarity and communication are essential for good relationships, productivity and keeping unnecessary anger to a minimum.

Support Groups

Have you ever asked a friend for advice about your work? Have you ever had someone lend you moral support while you worked to accomplish a goal? Perhaps someone "walked with you" as you went through a difficult time, such as firing an employee or getting through a difficult personal or work situation. If so, you know the strength and sense of confidence that comes through such support. One way of keeping such support in your life all the time is setting up an advisory support group for yourself. Many people do this informally and find it invaluable both for keeping them on a growth track and for helping them deal with difficulties as they arise. You can use two models for success:

1. Personal Board of Directors
2. Success groups

A University of Southern California survey of 302 bank employees found that workers who rated their job social scene as caring and friendly had higher self-esteem and less depression and anxiety than people employed in more hostile social climates.

Personal Board of Directors

This is the more formal of the two models. It gives you a group of people whose primary role is to react to your growth plan and to help you stay on track with it. Before you ask people to help you reach a goal, you must first have written down your

5

goals and objectives in the form of a mission statement, with time lines. Then, choose a group of five to eight people to meet with you regularly, once or twice a month.

It is important to have the group small enough that everyone can talk and large enough that you have a variety of experience and viewpoints. The value of such a group is that it helps you stay energized and committed in a way that working alone on the same goals often does not. Many new managers find this a great way to learn from more experienced people and to get support from outside their work circles.

Exercise

If you think having your own personal Board of Directors might be something you should try, think about this:

1. What qualities would be helpful to me in my board?

_____

_____

_____

2. What are the names of people I could invite who have one or more of these qualities?

_____

_____

_____

3. What is a realistic deadline for myself to have my board in place? _____

A personal Board of Directors functions as an expert advisory panel on the business of being you. As in any business, you must focus on what you want, identify your strengths and focus your energies on the best options. A personal Board of Directors provides insight, guidance and direction. It acts as a mentor for your success.

After sharing your plan with the "board," you use a simple two-step format for your meetings. (Many people find it convenient to meet for breakfast or lunch.) The first step is to report on what you have accomplished since the last meeting and what you will accomplish by the next meeting. The second step of each gathering is getting feedback and advice both on what you have accomplished and on what you intend to do.

Success Group

The second model is one that uses a small group of friends or peers. Again, six to eight people meet twice a month for about an hour and a half. This group agrees to meet for two months. During the first meeting each person explains what his goal is. It can be anything you are currently working toward in personal skill development, or it can be something at work. For example, sometimes it's dealing with a particular interpersonal problem on the job. Another time it might be completing a particular project. It's important to keep your goals simple and concrete, so that you can see progress in six to eight weeks.

A Three-Step Format

The format of the Success Group is very simple but demands a certain amount of discipline. Each person has 10 minutes to talk in turn. During that time he:

1. Reviews his goal.
2. Reports on his progress since the last meeting and explains what he will accomplish before the next meeting.
3. The final step is telling the group, "Here is what I need from you." Sometimes what you need is advice; sometimes it's information or networking. It could be that what you ask for may be to receive a phone call in a few days to get a friendly shove or to brainstorm on any obstacles you've met.

How workers cope with stress at work:
- *71% talk or joke with colleagues*
- *43% take coffee breaks*
- *37% walk at lunch time*
- *21% smoke*

5

If this format might be useful for you to try, think about this:

Exercise

What goal do I want to work toward within a group?

_____

_____

_____

Whom do I want to invite to be part of my success group?

_____

_____

_____

What is a realistic date to have this group in place? _____

Knowing you're not alone as you work toward your goals and as you deal with problems as they arise can, in itself, be empowering. These two models, one in which you receive help and the second in which you both give and receive help, are two tried and true examples of how to get help and support. Whether you use one of these methods or another model, the important thing is to set up structures for yourself that will give you what you need to grow and take care of yourself. Growth and self-care are important underpinnings for your personal development in dealing with conflict and anger.

Questions for Personal Development

1. What is the major emphasis of this chapter?

_____

_____

_____

_____

2. What are the most important things you learned from this chapter?

_____

_____

_____

_____

3. How can you apply what you learned to your current job?

_____

_____

_____

_____

4. How will you go about making these improvements?

_____

_____

_____

_____

5. How can you monitor improvement?

_____

_____

_____

_____

6. Summarize the changes you expect to see in yourself one year from now.

_____

_____

_____

_____

CHAPTER 6

Constructive Conflict

Did you ever have a conflict with a friend and then work through it successfully? It's likely that one of the things that helped you resolve it was the relationship you shared with that person. Because you knew each other well and cared about one another, the chances of working through the conflict were increased. If you had that same conflict with someone you hardly knew or someone you didn't have a positive relationship with, it would be unlikely that the problem could have been solved so readily.

Relationships play a key part in dealing with conflict. When you know a person and have shared something with her, when you both are striving to accomplish the same things, conflicts can be dealt with much more successfully. Relationships matter in your personal life and at work. Here are some principles for maintaining positive relationships during conflict. Some of these have been mentioned throughout the previous chapters, but they are brought together here to focus on the relationship dimension of your conflict management style.

6

> *"I don't know the key to success, but the key to failure is trying to please everybody."*
> Bill Cosby

Seven Principles for Positive Relationships During Conflict

1. **Build winners; voting builds losers.**

   A management style that builds winners cultivates positive relationships. Whenever a vote is taken, there are winners and there are losers. If a person feels like she's lost and someone else has won, the relationship is affected. It's amazing how people begin to keep track of who wins over a period of time and get caught up in the political process of keeping score.

   Does this mean voting should never be used? No. But when you are going to use it, assess the decision being made and assess what the ramifications will be on the relationships involved. During conflicts of low-level intensity, voting can be used most effectively because the people are problem-focused and don't have so much of themselves invested. But when you use voting during Stages Two and Three, it tends to actually escalate the conflict because of either/or thinking at that level. Ironically, often the mistake is made of using voting at these higher conflict levels, because sides and opinions are so easy to count when people are polarized.

   So, consider the consequences before you decide to vote:
   1. How will losers participate with the new majority?
   2. What effect will it have on relationships and morale?
   3. Can a vote be tabled long enough to meet and discuss alternatives with representatives?

2. **Declare a moratorium.**

   "Time-out" is a valuable tool during conflict. Relationships are more important than a decision. Time taken to build relationships and to search for a more acceptable outcome to the conflict can pay off in a healthy foundation that can tolerate more intense conflict in the future.

   When you use time as a valuable resource, however, it is important that you deliberately state your intentions and work behind the scenes to ensure the greatest possible outcome. For

> *"If you want an audience, start a fight."*
> Gaelic proverb

6

example, you could say:

- "We have some time; let's meet in small groups and look for alternatives."
- "No decision is worth hurt feelings. There are several people who have spent company time and proposed quality ideas. I want to find out why there is such diversity of opinion."
- "We're not ready to decide. A little more time invested now that we've seen the issues might help everyone."

Remember: Your follow-up after this is critical. Never "buy time" in this way and then neglect to take the action you promised.

3. **Encourage equal participation.**

Did you ever participate in a club as a member and then become an officer or leader in the group? No doubt that changed your commitment and sense of responsibility to the success of the club in a positive way. This same dynamic happens when we give people shared responsibility during conflict. Requiring a team effort for solving a problem decreases the likelihood of having it escalate to a Stage Three conflict, because its risk is seen. Here are some ways to have your team members share in the problem-solving responsibility and at the same time enrich and deepen their relationships:

1. Remind them that "we" are a team. Do this explicitly and then consistently refer to them as a team.
2. Get members to think like managers and look for creative responses that promote cooperation. In other words, give them the job of thinking through the possibilities, of coming up with new solutions.
3. Subdivide tasks. Do this in a way that creates barriers around areas of responsibility, and then give assignments that require cooperative efforts in order to cross those barriers. In this way people have to work as a team. What's more, they have now walked in someone else's shoes and have a new understanding of that person's perspective.

This kind of cross-functional team is viewed as essential by leading businesses today, not just during conflict management but during the creative process as well.

> *"Understanding how others view a conflict is knowledge that gives us strength. It enhances our ability to influence them."*
> Roger Fisher

6

"Nature has given us two ears but only one mouth."
Benjamin Disraeli

6

4. Actively listen.

Nothing builds trust and relationships better than sincere, involved listening skills. How do you do this? Primarily, stop talking. Listening skills are easy to learn if you're willing to practice. Listening is one of the most affirming things we can do for another person.

Listening affirms in several ways:
- Listening says, "You are important; I'll take time to hear what you have to say." Remember the last time that happened to you? How did it make you feel? How did you feel toward the listener?
- As a manager, listening gives you quick access to a perspective on the conflict as you hear what this person thinks and feels.
- It provides you with real data to help you make good decisions.
- Listening builds relationships. Any kind of sharing affects relationships, whether it is sharing food, time or ideas. A good self-test is to ask yourself after visiting with others: Did I gain as much information as I gave out?

5. Separate fact from fiction.

You know from your experience that no two people perceive the same event alike. When police officers interview witnesses at a traffic accident, they sometimes find it hard to believe people are even describing the same event. When someone is personally involved in an event, her perceptions are colored by many things: her experience, her emotional reaction to what happened, her history, her relationships with those involved, etc. Which story represents reality? As a manager you need to beware of "absolute" statements and challenge them.

At the same time it is important to encourage what is called "conditional truth." Conditional truth is when we agree to listen to every person before conditions are drawn or decisions made. It's the assumption that all people are accurate and their position is in the best interest of the company. Another approach is to be totally open to what each person says and assume that the person has good will. Differences result from varying perspectives rather than from lies. This is more of an attitude than a process, and you need to remind your group of this throughout the listening process.

It's important that you, the leader, take a firm role at this point. Facilitate good listening, then sort out perspectives that differ rather than challenge suspected liars. It's obvious that the latter simply escalates the conflict.

Finally, another benefit of separating fact from fiction is that it increases creativity in thinking and in looking for alternatives. When your workers are used to considering alternative perspectives, they are less likely to settle for easy answers, so you get a richer pool of ideas. After listening well, the effective manager instills a questioning attitude that looks for alternatives, not for debate.

"It's a rare person who wants to hear what he doesn't want to hear."
Dick Cavett

6. Separate the people from the problem.
Why is this so important? Because once the people and the problem become tangled, a problem becomes unmanageable. Is this easy to do? Surely you know from experience that it is not. Here are some ideas to help you separate the people from the problem:

- Talk in specific rather than general terms. Generalizations are open to misinterpretation and misunderstanding, and they do not move the issue forward. Clarity about your issues keeps the focus on the facts, not on the personalities.
- In Stage Two or Three, use concrete words. Help the group do this by asking for concrete clarification. Help the group stick to facts.
- Approach each conflicting party with a clean state and an open mind. Make no assumptions. Even if they assume you are aware of the conflict, have each party describe their version in its entirety. This gives you the chance to hear each perspective without either side having to defend their territory or stance. This helps those in conflict separate themselves from the event, at least for the moment.

6

153

- Create a safe environment. If you have an attitude that is calm and nonjudgmental, noncritical and open, you will help them resist their own fight-or-flight response that is natural when conflict escalates. When your people feel safe, they are less apt to stay in their entrenched positions. They become more open as they feel less threatened. Atmosphere is a major contributor to this.

7. Divide and conquer.

Something you may have noticed when your workers are involved in conflict is that, as the intensity of the conflict increases, people look for others who share their point of view and gravitate toward them. This polarization factor and the coalitions that emerge can be destructive in higher-level conflict. Factions form and then create a right/wrong and us/them atmosphere.

At the same time, no one wants to stand alone during an intense conflict. Everyone involved needs support from like-minded people. For this reason when you, as a manager, keep the language and notion of "team" very present during conflict, you can prevent destructive coalitions from forming. You need to frame the conflict as a team problem that needs to be solved.

At every turn, remind them of your expectations for them as a team. What you are striving for is to create a larger identity beyond individuals and coalitions, because when your workers feel they are part of something greater, it makes it harder for subgroups to form.

> *"Any fool can criticize, condemn and complain — and most fools do."*
> Benjamin Franklin

6

Five Don'ts of Conflict Management

There are some traps you can get caught in during conflict. Throughout this book you've been studying positive things to do to manage conflict and make it work for positive progress. Here are some pitfalls to avoid in your journey.

1. *Don't get into a power struggle.*

    Think about who you perceive as having authority over you. Why? Is it because of your respect for them or your fear of them? What is the source of that authority? Generally people will do what you want for one of two reasons: because you have power or because you have authority. It is generally acknowledged that as power increases, authority decreases, and as authority increases, power decreases.

    Power tends to be coercive; authority involves a sense of respect. Power tends to come from a position (you're my manager, you can fire me; you have on a police uniform, I'll stop my car when you say I should), whereas authority comes from proven competence for the leadership position (you're a good manager, you have shown you can lead us; you're my mentor, and I know I can trust your judgment).

6

Exercise

Who is someone you obey or follow because of power?

_____

Who is someone you obey or follow because of authority?

_____

As a manager you are a person with power. You may also have authority. Your authority can increase or decrease. It increases when you empower others without getting into power struggles with them.

In the normal course of your work life, as you enhance the power of others, their development will increase their commitment. This increased commitment impacts the power and the effectiveness of your whole team.

Sharing your power is similar to sharing the light of your candle with others. When you light another's candle, your light isn't decreased. In fact, there's more light for everybody. When you share power, this does not mean abdicating your leadership responsibility, but rather it means you're allowing others to take control of their feelings and of the task or issue in question. People need clearly defined norms and rules to function in a healthy and productive fashion. But, to be most effective during conflict, avoid power struggles. Here are some things you can do:

- Don't argue unless you are prepared to waste time.
- Don't engage in a battle unless you're prepared to lose, because you already have.
- Don't take total responsibility for others' emotions. As the one in control, share the responsibility.

2. *Don't become detached from the conflict.*
At first glance this may seem contradictory, but staying involved is a way to monitor conflict and to keep it under control. There are several factors at work here:

   a. As a manager you must be aware of the big picture and not get so wrapped up in the issue that you lose sight of the bigger picture.
   b. If you are so detached that you don't care, you can't follow any of the previous advice, nor can you contribute to the resolution. Excessive detachment also lessens your credibility and your ability to influence.
   c. Being involved also will help you learn about conflicts early on and manage them properly. The more you are engaged, the more likely you are to know what's going on and where the problems are.
   d. A passionate concern for the people and the problem is important if you are going to provide leadership. Contrary to management styles of the past, care and concern are not signs of

"Kindness is the noblest weapon to conquer with."
American proverb

6

weakness in the workplace; rather they are authentic human traits that call forth the best in all of us. A caring climate forms the best possible basis for dealing with conflicts that occur.

3. *Don't let conflict establish your agenda.*

This principle is especially important for new managers to recognize. It is a question of control. Do you need to handle conflict in a timely manner? Of course. Can you control when conflicts will occur? Of course not. But you need to be in control of your overall priorities and in control of how much time you consistently spend acting vs. reacting in your workplace. Conflict management, like all other management issues, requires that you keep your perspective focused on the direction and the goals of the company. Everything else you do — decisions, responses to conflict — must be consistent with this.

> *Do the important and delegate the urgent.*

Time management specialists remind us to "do the important and delegate the urgent." But under the pressure of conflict, sometimes managers ignore many important business matters. Sometimes urgent needs interfere with daily schedules. You need to look closely at how you are spending your time, to test whether you are managing the priorities and not managing conflict endlessly.

Here are some tips that can help you manage urgent issues:
- Don't spend all your time and energy on one issue.
- Watch time traps. Are there tasks that always seem to consume your time before you're aware it's gone?
- Identify urgent issues, especially negative or conflict issues. If you notice one consistent time offender, manage that offender.
  a. Are your people delegating up to you, getting you to do their work?
  b. When they bring you problems, do you also expect that they will have solutions to suggest?
  c. It's easy to get caught in the negative cycle of the "poor me" syndrome. Are those you manage in this cycle?

6

4. *Don't be caught "awfulizing."*

"Awfulizing," according to Joan Borysenko in *Minding the Body, Mending the Mind*, is "the tendency to escalate a situation into its worst possible conclusion." If you find yourself in a Stage Two or Stage Three conflict, it's fairly easy to be pushed to worst-case scenarios. People locked in an escalated conflict lose their ability to keep a perspective on the problem, because of the intensity of the emotions involved. Be aware of this, and don't allow your staff to succumb to exaggerating the consequences.

Here are some reminders that will help you avoid "awfulizing":
- People are rarely as benevolent as they perceive themselves to be.
- People are rarely as evil as their opponents perceive them to be.
- Individuals rarely spend much time thinking about the issues.
- The motivations of others are rarely as planned or thought out as they may appear to be. Most aspects of conflict arise from other events and are not the result of cold-hearted calculation.
- Every conflict has a history that extends beyond the present. The people and their previous patterns of relating are a part of the present perception.

5. *Don't be fooled by projection.*

Projection is an emotional release. People unconsciously project their own flaws and weaknesses onto others. During conflict, in order to be effective, you should notice the generalizations people are making and the accusations made about others. Particularly pay attention to comments about someone else's motivations. We may understand others, and we may be able to predict their actions accurately, but it is unfair and dangerous to believe anyone can read someone else's mind.

Here are some ways to manage projection:
- Focus the parties back on the facts. Sometimes listing the facts in writing helps everyone look at reality.
- When a generalization is made, require the person to be more specific. Is it true that the other person always

Conflict is healthy when it causes the parties to explore new ideas, tax their position and beliefs, and stretch their imagination.

6

does this? Is it accurate to say that the person has never done that? Ask for specific, concrete examples.

- When judgments are made about another's motivations, remind the speaker, "We don't know why Marvin wanted to do this protocol that particular way, but we can look at the facts of what happened."

The Seven Principles for Positive Relationships During Conflict and the Five Don'ts of Conflict Management are most effective when used by those who have a love for their company, their job and its people. It will be your relationships with people that will determine your success in managing conflict. Building positive relationships with others is an ongoing process that you need to attend to every day.

Here are three specific behaviors all parties should use to keep relationships open during problem-solving or conflict resolution:

1. **Be encouraging.** When you let others know that their ideas and feelings are important, you are more likely to receive the same kind of response from them.

2. **Be expressive of feelings.** If you're able to name your own feelings, you will be more clear and more clearly understood by others. In addition, your power is enhanced through this trust-building. Naming your feelings also helps others do the same.

3. **Be cooperative.** Cooperating is not the same as compromising; rather, it means being honest, direct and sincere about naming and solving the problem in the best manner possible. When each person is cooperative, she participates to the best of her ability in the work of the group at this moment.

> *"Kind words can be short and easy to speak but their echoes are truly endless."*
> Mother Teresa

6

Mutual Benefit Areas

The one perspective every skilled conflict manager employs is accessing the mutual benefit area. That's the zone of agreement conflicted parties share. For example, in the graphic below, the shaded area represents the area of disagreement. The white area is nonconflicted.

In any conflict, the conflicted area is always much smaller than the unconflicted. But the emotion, tension, anger and fear heighten the disagreement and create a disproportionate focus on the differences. In fact, research indicates that generally we have 15 percent that's conflicted and 85 percent that we already agree on.

Former President Jimmy Carter heightened the technique of mutual-benefit focusing during the Camp David Accords. He realized that the way to success and to reduce conflict is to get parties talking about the nonconflicted aspects first.

6

Former President Jimmy Carter heightened the technique of mutual-benefit focusing during the Camp David Accords. He realized that the way to success and to reduce conflict is to get parties talking about the nonconflicted aspects first. By simply turning away from the negative and sharing mutually beneficial aspects, both parties realized how much they have in common and how much both stood to lose.

Focusing on the mutual benefits looks like this:

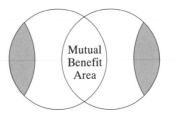

By simply turning parties toward the mutual points of agreement, opportunity arises to openly adjust the much smaller aspects of disagreement.

Nine Conflict Resolution Skills That Lead to Agreement

When you are a manager or supervisor, you are expected to be a leader for those who work for you. There is no time when your leadership is needed more than during conflict. As you develop your leadership and managerial abilities, here are nine skills you will continue to hone:

Angry people often fail to hear what others have to say.

1. **The ability to listen.** Management expert Tom Peters says that superior leaders have always been distinguished by the ability to connect through listening well. The ability to really hear what the other person is saying raises the profit margin as well as humanizes the workplace setting. Knowing how to listen well is an art, a creative act. It means listening with your eyes as well as your ears — that is, taking in body language, gestures and facial expression as well as words, tone and inflection.

   You do your best listening with your eyes open and your mouth closed. We have two ears and one mouth and should use them in that proportion, listening twice as much we talk. At the same time your mind must be open to take in what the person is saying rather than be busy formulating your response or judgment.

   At the very basic level, listening well means not doing anything else while the speaker is speaking. It is not selective hearing, filtering out what you don't want to hear. It is not finishing the speaker's sentence for her; it is not thinking you have to solve the problem she is describing. When you listen well you listen naively, that is, without pre-formed judgments.

   A great deal of so-called communication is two people talking at each other rather than an exchange of ideas and information. In conflict, you will find people practicing one-upmanship or engaging in a battle to win rather than attempting to learn and solve the problem.

6

2. **Be a role model.**   When asked how they learned their most important lessons or most valued traits, most people will tell you about someone whom they admired. That's what being a role model is — teaching through example. You do this when you show your employees the behavior you want from them. If you lose your temper, you are showing them that's how frustration is handled here. If you arrive late, treat people in a negative way or are disrespectful of others, those are the norms you're setting for them. All of us copy other people's behavior. In the workplace people model their boss. The most important modeling you can do is to stay positive. Negativity is highly contagious, and negativity by the person in charge will spread like a brush fire. Be a solution-oriented role model rather than a problem-centered one. That's what the people working for you will learn too.

Being a Role Model

What are the qualities you want your employees to have?

_____

_____

_____

_____

How do you think your employees would rate you on those qualities?

_____

Put a number next to each quality listed above, with one being the lowest and 10 the highest.

Choose one of the qualities you want to improve, and write it here:

_____

What will help you improve your own modeling of this for your staff?

_____

_____

_____

3. **The ability to initiate discussion and create feedback.** While these are not the same, they can be developed by asking questions. People love to talk about themselves as well as about things that affect them. As you ask questions about others, they will give you helpful feedback for your purposes. In addition, this dialogue is helpful in establishing the mutual benefit areas between individuals.

4. **The ability to make personal change.** In order to make personal change, you have to be willing to go outside your comfort zone. Remember, if you're not getting better, you're getting worse. Life doesn't stand still, and if you don't keep growing, you're not getting all you can out of life. Change is not necessarily easy. In fact, it can be very uncomfortable. We tend to get comfortable in particular habit patterns and then tend to stay there. But if you're prepared to go outside your comfort zone, you'll reap the great benefits of an enriched and more interesting life. You may not get encouragement to change, and you may even get resistance from those around you. People like the status quo, and when you change it affects them, too. When you expand your comfort zone, you leave some people behind and threaten others.

Do you know someone who discourages you from changing? It could be a small change ... or a big change, from trying a new cuisine to going on a trip, from taking a class to applying for a promotion. At best others may not support you and at worst try to keep you from moving ahead. The person who has to make the decision to change is you.

6

5. **The ability to be vigilant and persistent.** It's surprising to learn that most people fail when they're on the verge of success. In fact, 80 percent of all new sales are made after the fifth call on a client, but 48 percent of salespeople make only one call. Twenty-five percent of all sales come only after the second call and 12 percent not until after the third call. Only 10 percent of salespeople keep calling until they succeed. No wonder so few are highly successful. As in sales, persistence in conflict management pays off, but people almost always quit before they experience success. There's a fine line between blind commitment to a point that cannot change and persistent tenacity toward a satisfactory agreement. One of the easiest ways to tell the difference is to know whether you are gathering debate points or seeking mutually beneficial results.

> *"It is not true that life is one damn thing after another ... it's the same damn thing over and over again."*
> Edna St. Vincent Millay

163

> *"Anxiety is the rust of life, destroying its brightness and weakening its power."*
> Tyron Edwards

6. **The ability to deal with fear.** Have you ever faced something you really feared and felt the joy, exhilaration and confidence that came from facing it? Did you ever stand frightened on the end of a diving board? Do you remember the first time you drove a car? Perhaps your challenge was giving a speech in public or taking on a new assignment at work. Whatever the situation, when you reflect on it, you know that the best way to deal with fear is to face it. Ask yourself: What's the worst thing that can happen? Can I survive that? What's the best thing that can happen? Isn't it worth the risk? Fear itself can't hurt you, but not facing it can result in failure. Whatever happens, you will have learned something and, most importantly, you will have the great satisfaction of knowing that you didn't run away from what you feared.

It takes courage for managers to handle conflict. Stepping up to the challenge with your new knowledge and skill is worth the risk. It's the only way you have to learn how to deal with conflict.

7. **The ability to facilitate others.** Some people will watch and wait until others take the first step before trying something. These people are called followers. They are looking to others to set an example and model behavior. An important part of your work in conflict management is helping followers move forward. By helping others participate in resolving conflict, you help yourself. The benefits to you are increased experience, confidence and self-knowledge because, as you facilitate others, you are also refining your own conflict resolution skills.

8. **A dedication to continued education.** This relates to No. 4. Education is a way to grow and change and stretch yourself. There is both formal and informal education: Formal includes course work, seminars, etc., while informal includes learning from others, such as mentors or peers, and learning from situations. Remember that the road of life is a toll road, and it's always under construction. Make sure you know where you want to go on it, and keep yourself moving ahead. If you don't, you're liable to get run over from behind.

9. **The ability to utilize resources.** If you look at a person's friends, you will learn a lot about the person herself. If you make a list of the people with whom you spend a lot of time, you can tell a lot about yourself. Do you associate with people who will help you or people who hold you back? Do you associate with learners? Do you associate with those who are like what you want to become? Resources come in many forms. The most important are people, so it's helpful to join professional organizations. You can also set aside a reading time at home or at work or one evening a week in the library. You can attend workshops, listen to tapes and, most importantly, you can set goals for yourself and budget time to make them happen. Remember, invest in time rather than waste it.

Intervention

The airline pilot has power at her fingertips: Millions of dollars in equipment and hundreds of lives are at stake with every movement. Behind the scenes is a flight crew, less visible to the general public but just as responsible. There is also a ground control crew as well as a control tower crew. Further removed is a cadre of company officials, travel agents and airport staff who provide a multitude of services.

It's easy to praise the pilot for a pleasurable flight, but without thousands of other people, a positive end result would be impossible.

This analogy applies equally to conflict management. An effective intervention strategy begins with the humble awareness that "superhuman" skills are inadequate without the cooperation of others—so teamwork is essential to effective conflict management, especially once conflict escalates to higher levels.

The good manager develops her skills and is confident about what she can do. The good manager is also clear about what she cannot do alone. When conflict escalates to its highest levels, negotiation and mediation need to be used. If this is the case, an intervention team is brought in from outside the conflicting groups. This team is not necessarily from outside the company, but it needs to meet several criteria:

> *"Let our advance worrying become advance thinking and planning."*
> Winston Churchill

6

165

Qualities of an Intervention Team

1. It must have the skill, competence and experience to deal with high-level-conflict.

2. It must have the authority it needs to carry out its work.

3. It must be perceived by both parties as authoritative and capable of dealing fairly with all the issues.

4. It must have been chosen through a process in which both parties participated.

The presence of an intervention team is evidence that things have escalated beyond the workable stage. Events must be controlled by an external source. The following guidelines can be helpful in establishing the intervention team.

Guidelines for an Intervention Team

1. *Limit hostility.* There is little need for hostility once the intervention team is selected. Its presence is an indication that the lines of conflict are severely drawn. A deliberate de-escalation of hostility by the intervention team can be helpful in moving the conflict to more manageable stages.

2. *Become involved.* The intervention team is capable of providing insight and creative alternatives. Lower-level conflict requires participation in the final outcome. Once Stage Three conflict has been reached, resolution is essential. Ownership in a negotiated or mediated settlement comes when the intervention team steps out of the picture.

3. *Get a note-taker.* The intervention team should secure an accurate note-taker rather than do this itself. The attention necessary to record the details can distract from efforts to resolve the conflict.

"A problem well stated is a problem half solved."
Charles F. Kettering

4. *Keep explanations brief.* The intervention team will provide feedback during the process. This is a time for clear, clean, crisp and factual reporting, not for speeches or lengthy explanations.

5. *Shun confidentiality.* The intervention team will not promise confidentiality. To do so could inhibit its effectiveness. In addition, during Stage Three conflicts, people will tend to "tone down" threats and accusations when confidentiality is not guaranteed. When they do this, the mood of the conflict is de-escalated.

> *During high-level conflict it is typical for people to exaggerate issues and facts.*

6. *Avoid being a rescuer.* Once a team has been identified, there can be a tendency to expect it to take on the responsibility for solving problems and rescuing the company. All the team can do is offer a third-party perspective. It is easy to promise more than can be delivered during conflict management. High expectations can put pressure on the team rather than on the disputing parties, where it belongs. They are the ones still responsible for resolving the conflict.

7. *Begin an accountability process.* During high-level conflict it is typical for people to exaggerate issues and facts. The team must insist on accuracy of statements about people and about issues. The intervention team must be willing to confront exaggerated positions and ask if an individual is willing to be quoted on such a point.

6

8. *Deal with rumors or accusations directly.* By generating face-to-face dialogue, the team can help control unsubstantiated statements. Remember the technique described in an earlier chapter:
   - Ask if the individual is willing to go with you and face the other person.
   - If she refuses, ask if you can quote her to the accused person.
   - If she refuses, state categorically that there is no point in addressing this issue any further and that you will not give it any credence.

Remember that while an effective intervention team can be a catalyst for high-level conflict, the success or failure resides with the parties involved. Here is a five-stage process for a team to use in third-party intervention.

1. Establish the parameters.
2. Collect the data.
3. Frame the issues.
4. Generate alternatives.
5. Evaluate and agree.

Intervention: A Five-Stage Mediation Process

Stage 1: Establish the parameters

"Never mistake motion for action."
Ernest Hemingway

Did you ever watch a group of 10-year-olds working on a project or playing a game together? They typically spend much of their time arguing about what the rules are and who broke or kept them, rather than playing or working together. Any event, whether friendly or hostile, has rules to follow. Whether it's attending a dinner party, playing on a soccer team or participating in an auction, when the rules are clear in advance, our focus can be on the process so we can accomplish what we're there to do. At high-level conflict, clarity about the "rules of the game" is critical. This helps set a positive tone at the outset and gives the team credibility. Later, if a rule needs to be enforced, it can be done impersonally, because everyone was aware of it up front.

6

Basic Rules

1. Everyone is asked to speak in first-person terms, to use "I" statements rather than to blame or attack others by using "you" statements.

   Rationale: The goal of the intervention team is not to place blame but to find a solution.

2. Statements that contain assumptions about others will be accepted with skepticism.

   Rationale: The intervention team is looking for facts that are verifiable, not assumptions, gossip, etc. Once a statement is made, the team will seek to verify it and confirm or deny it.

3. Nothing should be said to the team that cannot be shared or verified.

   Rationale: Confidentiality leads to inside information that divides the group. This kind of activity is counterproductive to resolution. Work hard to keep everything on the record.

4. Threats are not acceptable.

   Rationale: The fact that an intervention team exists indicates that serious problems exist. Excessive hostility undermines resolution.

5. The intervention team acts as a catalyst.

   Rationale: Problems must be solved by those embroiled in the conflict. The intervention team has an outside perspective that can be helpful.

6. The team conducts interviews, distributes questionnaires and holds public information meetings as needed.

   Rationale: Everyone will be kept informed. Conflicting parties will be asked to stop all comments until the findings are completed by the team. At this point, the ones to talk with are the team members, not others.

6

> *"Listening means, first, giving attention ... If you concentrate, who knows? You might learn something."*
> Dorothy Carnegie

Stage 2: Collect the data

The work of gathering information about the conflict needs to happen in a short amount of time. The parties involved can provide an initial list of contacts who can give the following information:

- History of the conflict
- Patterns of communications
- A picture of how power is perceived to be distributed
- The priority of this problem in relation to the goals of the company or unit

This information can be gathered through a questionnaire and in personal interviews.

The success of the interview can easily be determined by the skill of the interviewer at using listening techniques. The interview should be characterized by fairness, objectivity, empathy and openness. It is important to provide nonverbal reassurance and support. This can reduce anxiety and move toward acceptance of events by parties on both sides.

"Conflict listening" is a specific listening skill that provides support to the speaker and at the same time clarifies feelings and content and helps them separate the two. As the chart below illustrates, this is a two-step process in which the interviewer first defuses the emotions and then reframes the issues:

Conflict Listening

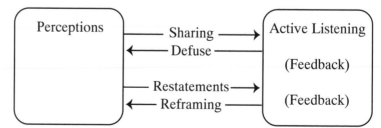

Reprinted with permission from *How to Manage Conflict*, page 54, by Dr. William Hendricks, copyright 1991, National Press Publications, Overland Park, KS.

Step one: Defuse.

This step is designed to allow the interviewer to hear everything the individual brings to the conflict. Many emotions, some of them heightened, are present and must be sifted through. The interviewer engages in active listening and then reflects back what has been said, toning down, or defusing, the emotions.

In some cases emotions will subside once the person has been heard.

Step two: Reframe.

In reframing, the interviewer synthesizes the individual's perceptions, balanced by the interviewer's perspectives. For example, "It sounds like things are really piling up and you feel overwhelmed. You'd like to do a good job, but feel like you are stepping behind. Am I right?" The goal here is to separate the people from the problem in whatever was said. In some cases emotions will subside once the person has been heard. In other cases the person will be unwilling or unable to let this separation happen. In this case, reframing is impossible. Throughout these interviews, interviewers are looking for the core issues. These won't be the same for everyone involved.

Stage 3: Frame the issues

The third stage in moving toward mediation is to frame the issues. Unlike in the previous stage, this step takes place in the public arena. The intervention team frames the issues it has identified and offers a wide range of options for consideration.

Remember that the intervention team members are not passive in this process. They've been brought in because the parties involved in the dispute can't settle the dispute alone. The team's role is to suggest a solution that meets the needs of the group and to encourage movement toward a positive outcome. The opposing parties need to move toward points of view that will converge.

Stage 4: Generate alternatives

Conflicts that have escalated to Stage Three are seldom single-issue disagreements. There are typically numerous points of contention, with people holding varying degrees of agreement and disagreement. One of the first things the team can do is move the group away from polarization by listing all the points of agreement. Sometimes the parties are surprised to discover they have some things in common, and discovering points of agreement can begin to lessen hostility.

6

At this point there is a change in atmosphere. It shifts from being intervention-controlled to group-controlled. Although the team presents several ideas initially, the floor is gradually opened to input from the group. The intervention team can use as one of its options a worst-case scenario. This picture can be shocking and have the effect of dramatically shifting the group toward wanting to work out a more agreeable solution.

If negative and reactionary feelings arise at this point, the team must be willing to stop all input with a quick comment such as, "That has been heard, and we have attempted to deal with it in our presentations. Please help us focus on the future now." Alternatives continue to be elicited until ideas have run out. At this point the team calls for a break.

Typically the entire group moves to a new setting, an entirely different room for this part of the process. The group should be seated at a circular table to avoid the "us" and "them" feel that can come from facing the opposition across the table.

Now the intervention team provides very specific and direct leadership. The team works with the easy issues first. The reason for this is that, when the group members experience small successes, they begin to invest in making progress. They start to feel invested in an outcome and are energized to continue making progress. Once the easy concessions have been defined, the core issues can be addressed.

Dealing with the core issues, those that present the major discord, is not easy. The team must be open to all points of view, and gradually some people will feel that a new group has formed: a "we" instead of "us" and "them." As this happens, the new direction in which the group is moving is felt to be "our" territory, not "their" territory. It removes the sense that "we" have lost and "they" have won. If this doesn't happen and the process breaks down, worst-case scenarios can be presented again.

Last-resort options are voting on alternatives and compromise. When voting occurs, one side wins and the other loses. Everyone must clearly understand before voting that whoever loses must comply with the outcome of the vote. Generally, compromise is more appealing than voting.

"A fanatic is one who can't change his mind and won't change the subject."
Winston Churchill

6

The reason compromise is left as a last resort is that in compromise, no one wins. In compromise solutions, there are "almost winners" and "almost losers." It is rare to have much emotional commitment to such a solution. Compromise is perceived as a tie, and so there is not a clear sense of satisfaction. Yet, compromise may be better than losing everything!

Whatever solution results, it must still be presented to those outside this group, and that needs to be done by the intervention team and the spokespersons in a public manner.

In compromise solutions, there are "almost winners" and "almost losers."

Stage 5: Evaluate and agree

Care needs to be taken to make the public presentation well. The message that the team and the spokespersons want to communicate is, "This is a great alternative to our problem." In order to do this, the spokespersons are not allowed to speak privately to their own group. A representative from the intervention team and spokespersons from all factions must be seen together as a group at the front of the room, giving a united front and explaining the conclusions together.

The team leader should have drafted a letter of consensus, which lists in a positive manner the conclusions that have been reached. This letter includes three areas:
1. We met ...
2. We discussed ...
3. We did ...

6

Management's "Alongside" Strategy

During the intervention team's work, management should have developed an "alongside" strategy for business, which provides time to work with people across the barriers that had developed. Here are some components of such a plan:

1. Focus on the big picture by identifying to all parties that the company is bigger than this conflict. It should foster an attitude that work will continue and promote the expectation that people will work together.

2. Find ways to generate meaningful teamwork and work toward some immediate team success in short-term goals.

3. Parties that are entrenched in Stage Three should be identified and given short-term, easy-to-complete tasks. This builds confidence and provides opportunities to suggest that, until the conflict is settled favorably for everyone, the risk of extensive involvement in team projects and goals would be unwise.

Classic Dispute Resolution Models

When conflict arises in our personal life, in our society, between and among workers, in our neighborhood or anywhere, there are a limited number of options for how to settle the dispute.

As you read the headlines or catch the evening news, you're likely to hear the following: A coup takes place and a politician is put in jail; a neighborhood group meets with the police department to discuss a chronic problem; a Supreme Court ruling on a case is announced; someone is shot in an argument over a parking space; an airline strike is settled. What do these scenarios share? They each contain the story of a conflict handled in a different way, reasonably or violently.

When conflict arises in our personal life, in our society, between and among workers, in our neighborhood or anywhere, there are a limited number of options for how to settle the dispute. The chart on the next page outlines what those options are. There is a wide range of things to do, and there is a wide spectrum of control, within the process itself. Sometimes the individual has little or no control as, for example, when there is a violent overthrow of government. At the other end of the spectrum, such as when you merely disagree with a situation but choose to either tolerate it or walk away, you have a lot of personal control. In the classic resolution models, the farther up the ladder you go, the less control you have. As noted earlier, that's one of the reasons it's important to settle disputes at the lowest possible level of conflict. That's when you have the most control over your options.

6

Classic Dispute Resolution Models

Violence

Nonviolent Overthrow

Legislation

Court
(imposed third party)

Arbitration

Mediation
(voluntary third party)

Negotiation
(management skills)

Discussion
(problem-solving skills)

Toleration
(coping skills)

Reprinted with permission from "How to Handle Conflict and Manage Anger," page 20, copyright 1992, Rockhurst College Continuing Education Center, Inc., Overland Park, KS.

In the top box, which includes violence, nonviolent overthrow and legislation, only legislation gives you much control. If this involves a representative system, sometimes you can effect change, but it takes time. In the middle box, which includes going to court (where you have an imposed third party), arbitration and mediation, in which you have a voluntary third party, you can sometimes choose the resources and sometimes not. In all of these models, there is more control imposed than in the previous examples.

Finally, in the lowest box are negotiation, discussion and tolerance. Here you can choose to take on increased personal responsibility. In negotiation you use your management skills, in discussion you are calling on your skills of problem-solving and, at the level of toleration, you are making use of coping skills.

In negotiation you use your management skills, in discussion you are calling on your skills of problem-solving and, at the level of toleration, you are making use of coping skills.

6

You can become more and more skilled at dealing with lower levels of conflict, so that the other types will rarely, if ever, need to be employed.

All of the tools mentioned here are important and appropriate to use at certain times. Obviously, not all of them can be used in every situation. What works at lower levels of conflict, such as problem-solving, certainly is ineffective when conflict escalates to the point of going to court. Likewise if someone has become so angry over a conflict that she is at the point of resorting to violence, tolerance is not the method to employ! You can become more and more skilled at dealing with lower levels of conflict, so that the other types will rarely, if ever, need to be employed. The key to doing this is for you to practice what you have learned. And that is your responsibility. What will help you with this growth task? Who can help you with it?

6

Questions for Personal Development

1. What is the major emphasis of this chapter?

_____

_____

_____

_____

2. What are the most important things you learned from this chapter?

_____

_____

_____

_____

3. How can you apply what you learned to your current job?

_____

_____

_____

_____

4. How will you go about making these improvements?

_____

_____

_____

_____

5. How can you monitor improvement?

_____

_____

_____

_____

6. Summarize the changes you expect to see in yourself one year from now.

_____

_____

_____

_____

6

6

Summary

Conflict distorts facts, heightens emotions and challenges professional relationships. As a final summary, the seven Cs of conflict management offer an alternative to conflict, fear and anger.

The Seven Cs of Conflict Management

1. **Characteristics.** Every conflict has specific characteristics. As discussed in Chapter 1, it is possible to understand how conflict and anger work. This understanding, in itself, gives you tremendous power in the face of conflict, whether it occurs in your personal life or in a work situation. You have also debunked the myths that commonly surround conflict and therefore need not fall victim to their power. Now you are free to explore the territory of the specific conflict. You can more confidently and competently chart the unknown waters of conflict.

2. **Classification.** Another source of power and confidence is the understanding that conflicts can be classified. As explained in Chapter 2, there are different types of conflicts: intrapersonal and interpersonal. Understanding that conflict can be classified this way enables you to see that by compartmentalizing it, you have the ability to deal with conflict in a systematic way. An understanding of the stages of conflict described in the same chapter frees you to immediately clarify what level of conflict you are dealing with and thus know what kind of response to use. Stage One conflict calls on your coping skills, Stage Two requires your management skills and in a Stage Three conflict, you need outside resources for intervention.

> *"To make no mistakes is not in the power of man; but from their errors and mistakes the wise and good learn wisdom for the future."*
> Plutarch

179

> *If both sides walk away from your negotiation feeling positive, progress has been made.*

3. **Constructive.** Positive actions are the best response to negative events. As Chapter 3 describes, you can be constructive during destructive events. Good managers are productive, even during conflict! The tools in this chapter will give you many, many options for positive action.

4. **Credibility.** Chapters 3 and 4 help you enhance your credibility as a manager by addressing issues in a thoughtful and consistent manner. One goal during conflict management is to create credibility by matching modern business strategies with conflict management strategies. Your conflict management style must be not only proactive but consistent with your normal style of management, if you are to have credibility.

5. **Conditional.** No two conflicts are the same. The same dispute in another place or even in the same place with different parties is quite different. People change. Issues change. Throughout this book you have found ways to develop a variety of skills so that you can adapt to the changing dynamics of your business situation. Chapter 2 really opened up our options so we are not stuck with one style or mode of thinking.

> *As a workplace manager, you cannot solve social problems, but you can help your employees learn to deal with anger and conflict appropriately within the work context.*

6. **Care.** One of the messages in Chapters 5 and 6 is that, to the extent that you care for yourself and for the relationships with your workers, your job of dealing with conflict is eased. Caring about your company and its mission is another essential ingredient.

    In Chapter 5 and Chapter 6, caring for yourself and showing your team how important that is was discussed because emotional health and positive relationships and skills are the underpinnings of handling conflict.

7. **Constraint.** Finally, Chapter 6 discusses the need for external resources in order to keep things in perspective. The constraint factor encourages you to use an intervention team when conflict escalates to threatening levels.

Conclusion

Competition of "Goods"

If conflict was always a battle between good and evil, our work in managing it would be easier. But life is not that simple, and conflicts are not black and white. If you get phone calls from two different headhunters each offering you a job that meets all your dreams, you may experience both elation and conflict. Choosing between them is not selecting good over evil, it's selecting good over good. Sometimes settling conflict is sorting out from among competing "goods." Competition between two elements that are both good can happen at the same level between peers, or it can occur between levels of the organization.

Peer-Level Conflict

Perhaps two workers who are peers disagree over what should be done regarding a specific project. What each of them is fighting for is a good outcome, but the process each has chosen is totally different. This is one kind of competition of goods. In this case, using the information you've received throughout this book will facilitate resolution, especially if you handle it at a lower level. As you define the problem apart from the people involved, it is helpful to remind both sides that this is not a battle between good and evil or right over wrong but a competition of goods. This will help them work toward alternative options in a manner that is as objective as possible.

"Those who never retract their opinions love themselves more than they love truth."
Joseph Joubert

Interlevel Conflict

In this instance what is good for one level of the organization is in conflict with what's good for another level. What is good for the individual may be in conflict with what is good for the department. What is good for the department may conflict with the common good of the company.

Conflict of "Goods"

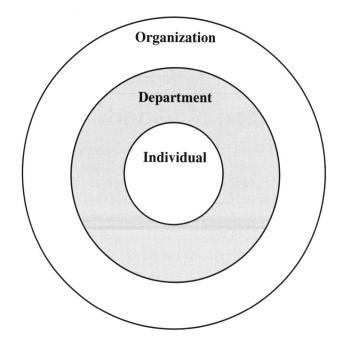

While the needs of each level have to be met so that each can contribute to the overall success of the organization, every solution should support the bigger objectives of the company.

If you look at the conflict issues in relation to the organization as a whole, it will help you develop the most satisfactory solution. Using the simple graphic above helps situate both the conflict and the possible solutions. Who is impacted by what each side wants? Whose interests are involved? Asking these kinds of questions helps you to more clearly determine the fallout and the implications of each of the options presented, so that no part is shortchanged. Looking at your conflict in this manner reminds you again of the critical importance of having clarity about the goals and priorities of the organization as a whole. While the needs of each level have to be met so that each can contribute to the overall success of the organization, every solution should support the bigger objectives of the company.

Maturity in Management

When we are born, we are totally helpless. We can only cry and suck, and we are totally at the mercy of our parents to provide us with food, clothing, shelter and care. All we can do is take from them. As a child grows through the years, he grows and develops his skills and capacities. As this happens he becomes more self-sufficient. The child who learns to walk is less dependent. The child who learns to read takes another step toward independence. As time goes on and he can spread his wings socially and his world expands from the cocoon of the family, he becomes more and more independent. Independence is the primary goal for parents and for maturing young adults. It is often associated with maturity. And indeed, learning to cope with life and becoming self-sufficient and personally skilled are critical steps in the development of a human being.

Independence, however, is not maturity. The mature person, though capable of "taking care" of herself, realizes that at best she is not independent, but interdependent. Interdependence allows us to learn from others, to show our vulnerability, to contribute to others and to accomplish so much more than we can alone. Having the maturity to be interdependent requires that we can sometimes bend rather than be rigid, be open to another's ideas when we feel we are right, and to share in the joys and sorrows that come from working cooperatively. Interdependence makes us able to stand outside ourselves, see things through the eyes of another and to learn from that. It challenges us to see the bigger picture and to value not just what is good for me but what is good for us, for the common good.

This kind of mature interdependence is enormously valuable in dealing with conflict. It enables us to:
1. Really listen to one another.
2. Show our feelings.
3. Separate the person from the problem.
4. Value the big picture.
5. Work for the common good.

> *"Our fatigue is often caused not by work, but by worry, frustration and resentment."*
> Dale Carnegie

Throughout this book each of these five skills has been addressed in theory and in practice. As you develop your maturity and skill, the more you will become an effective manager, a more complete, mature human being and a happier and more fulfilled person.

Remember, your goal is not to do away with conflict or to create a false peace by not allowing conflict to be expressed or acknowledged. Your goal is conflict utilization, that is, managing conflict so that positive and important growth occurs. Your goal is to acknowledge and deal with the substance of the conflict in a way that cares for the relationship between the parties. The relationship needs not only to be maintained but also enhanced through the process. What people in conflict want is to know that their interests have been met through publicly addressing the issue, to feel that the process was fair and to feel psychological satisfaction.

As a manager you have a great opportunity with each conflict because, when you look at conflict, you see opportunity. You have the knowledge and tools to be a new kind of leader in the workplace. Good luck!

> *"We may have all come on different ships, but we're in the same boat now."*
> Dr. Martin Luther King Jr.

184

Index

YOUR BACK-OF-THE-BOOK STORE

ORDER FORM

Because you already know the value of National Press Publications Desktop Handbooks and Business User's Manuals, here's a time-saving way to purchase more career-building resources from our convenient "bookstore."

- IT'S EASY … Just make your selections, then visit us on the Web, mail, call or fax your order. (See back for details.)
- INCREASE YOUR EFFECTIVENESS … Books in these two series have sold more than two million copies and are known as reliable sources of instantly helpful information.
- THEY'RE CONVENIENT TO USE … Each handbook is durable, concise and filled with quality advice that will last you all the way to the boardroom.
- YOUR SATISFACTION IS 100% GUARANTEED. Forever.

60-MINUTE TRAINING SERIES™ HANDBOOKS

TITLE	RETAIL PRICE*	QTY.	TOTAL
8 Steps for Highly Effective Negotiations #424	$14.95		
Assertiveness #4422	$14.95		
Balancing Career and Family #4152	$14.95		
Common Ground #4122	$14.95		
The Essentials of Business Writing #4310	$14.95		
Everyday Parenting Solutions #4862	$14.95		
Exceptional Customer Service #4882	$14.95		
Fear & Anger: Control Your Emotions #4302	$14.95		
Fundamentals of Planning #4301	$14.95		
Getting Things Done #4112	$14.95		
How to Coach an Effective Team #4308	$14.95		
How to De-Junk Your Life #4306	$14.95		
How to Handle Conflict and Confrontation #4952	$14.95		
How to Manage Your Boss #493	$14.95		
How to Supervise People #4102	$14.95		
How to Work With People #4032	$14.95		
Inspire and Motivate: Performance Reviews #4232	$14.95		
Listen Up: Hear What's Really Being Said #4172	$14.95		
Motivation and Goal-Setting #4962	$14.95		
A New Attitude #4432	$14.95		
The New Dynamic Comm. Skills for Women #4309	$14.95		
The Polished Professional #4262	$14.95		
The Power of Innovative Thinking #428	$14.95		
The Power of Self-Managed Teams #4222	$14.95		
Powerful Communication Skills #4132	$14.95		
Present With Confidence #4612	$14.95		
The Secret to Developing Peak Performers #4962	$14.95		
Self-Esteem: The Power to Be Your Best #4642	$14.95		
Shortcuts to Organized Files and Records #4307	$14.95		
The Stress Management Handbook #4842	$14.95		
Supreme Teams: How to Make Teams Work #4303	$14.95		
Thriving on Change #4212	$14.95		
Women and Leadership #4632	$14.95		

MORE FROM OUR BACK-OF-THE-BOOK STORE
Business User's Manuals — Self-Study, Interactive Guide

TITLE	RETAIL PRICE	QTY.	TOTAL
The Assertive Advantage #439	$26.95		
Being OK Just Isn't Enough #5407	$26.95		
Business Letters for Busy People #449	$26.95		
Coping With Difficult People #465	$26.95		
Dealing With Conflict and Anger #5402	$26.95		
Hand-Picked: Finding & Hiring… #5405	$26.95		
High-Impact Presentation and Training Skills #4382	$26.95		
Learn to Listen #446	$26.95		
Lifeplanning #476	$26.95		
The Manager's Role as Coach #456	$26.95		
The Memory System #452	$26.95		
Negaholics® No More #5406	$26.95		
Parenting the Other Chick's Eggs #5404	$26.95		
Taking AIM On Leadership #5401	$26.95		
Prioritize, Organize: Art of Getting It Done 2nd ed. #4532	$26.95		
The Promotable Woman #450	$26.95		
Sex, Laws & Stereotypes #432	$26.95		
Think Like a Manager 3rd ed. #4513	$26.95		
Working Woman's Comm. Survival Guide #5172	$29.95		

SPECIAL OFFER: Orders over $75 receive **FREE SHIPPING**	**Subtotal** — $ **Add 7% Sales Tax** *(Or add appropriate state and local tax)* — $ **Shipping and Handling** *($3 one item; 50¢ each additional item)* — $ **Total** — $ *VOLUME DISCOUNTS AVAILABLE — CALL 1-800-258-7248*

Name_____ Title_____

Organization _____

Address _____

City _____ State/Province _____ ZIP/Postal Code _____

Payment choices:

❏ Enclosed is my check/money order payable to National Seminars.

❏ Please charge to: ❏ MasterCard   ❏ VISA   ❏ American Express

Signature _____ Exp. Date _____ Card Number _____

❏ Purchase Order #_____

MAIL: Complete and mail order form
with payment to:
National Press Publications
P.O. Box 419107
Kansas City, MO 64141-6107

PHONE:
Call toll-free **1-800-258-7248**

INTERNET: www.natsem.com

FAX:
1-913-432-0824

Your VIP No.: 922-008438-099

08/01